Go & See

See what you have.
Invest all you've been given.

Jaclyn M. Loween

WESTBOW
PRESS®
A DIVISION OF THOMAS NELSON
& ZONDERVAN

WestBow Press books may be ordered through booksellers or by contacting:

WestBow Press
A Division of Thomas Nelson & Zondervan
1663 Liberty Drive
Bloomington, IN 47403
www.westbowpress.com
844-714-3454

ISBN: 978-1-6642-1026-4 (sc)
ISBN: 978-1-6642-1025-7 (e)

Library of Congress Control Number: 2020921087

Print information available on the last page.

WestBow Press rev. date: 01/19/2021

Table of Contents

Lesson 5

Lesson 6

Lesson 7

Lesson 8

Closing

Small Group Guide: Tips & Lesson by Lesson Instructions

What People are Saying About Experiencing *Go & See*.

Go & See continues to change my life on a daily basis as I realized by reading and studying the words that God has a very specific plan to use me just the way I am. I was able to see that my past has positively shaped me into the person my spouse, kids, coworkers, family and friends need in their lives. We are all uniquely designed and having a better understanding of our purpose gives true life!

~ Jamie DeBoer (*Go & See* retreat participant and co-founder of *True North Pursuit*)

Go & See for me was a guided journey of intentionally sitting with the Lord. The tools, exercises, assessments, and questions invited me to look at the pieces of my life to see how God made me and how I can live on purpose in this season. Jaclyn has poured her heart into crafting each page to be worthwhile, helpful, and most importantly, centered on God's Word.

~ Katy Zitzman (*Go & See* retreat participant and children's ministry leader, Harvest Church)

Every single time I sat down and found a quiet place to read, *Go & See* was exactly what I needed. It brought me closer to God and helped me out of burnout, steadying me to face the next season of my life. This is for everyone wondering what to do with their life. This is for those who have lost their passion. Who feel trapped by confusion and weariness. Who feel like they're going through the motions. It's for those who have so much passion they don't know what to do with it. For those who want to change the world but don't know where to start. For those who want to know how their mundane life can glorify God and have meaning.

~ S. G. Willoughby (Author of *He's Making Diamonds*; Founder of the Diamonds Conference)

Jaclyn Loween has created a powerful resource for anyone wanting to discover their full purpose and walk in their godly destiny! This book provides a journey of reflection, discovery, and practical application. It inspires the reader to uncover the meaning and values embedded in their life stories and to share stories of God's faithfulness with the next generation. Great to read as an individual or with a small group!

~ Jolene Erlacher, Ed.D (Author of *Millennials in Ministry*, *Daniel Generation* and founder of Leading Tomorrow: Strategies for a New Generation)

Go & See helped me realize the importance my own personal story holds as well as how to evaluate my gifts and how to use both for God's glory. Go and see is a powerful tool for discipleship!

~ Ashley Cole (*Go & See* retreat participant, mom and hobby farmer)

I cannot wait to share this resource with people in my life! Jaclyn inspired me to dig deeper and really explore my Identity in HIM and by understanding who God made me to be, it has helped me to love others better and with more compassion. This wonderful resource that has not only impacted my life but the lives of those around me.

~ Nichole Giese (*Go & See* retreat participant, mom and farmers' wife)

Go & See takes the reader on a journey into their spiritual past and future. By reflecting on what and who has shaped our spiritual past and inspiring us to use our spiritual gifts, Jaclyn Loween illuminates the plan that God has for each of us.

~ Jennifer Klecker (Attorney at Law, mom and fellow-runner)

If you've ever wondered what your life has to offer and how you can share that, take this adventure of searching with the Lord and allowing Jaclyn's passion to equip you with the tools in this book and help extract from your own life the gifts, talents, and dreams that are already in you to share with others.

~ Adell Lukes (*Go & See* retreat participant, mom, and writer)

Go & See is a great step-by-step guide and resource to help people who are serious about and committed to discovering their unique purpose--ready to learn ways to partner with the Holy Spirit to excavate their past, embrace their present, and recognize their unique gifts so they can step into the future with clarity and confidence to live out their God-given purpose and vision.

~ Natalie Dawn Hanson (Founder of the Made to Soar Movement and author of, *Made to Soar: Christ-Centered Truths to Encourage, Equip, & Empower Moms*)

Thank You for Embarking on This Journey

Dear Reader,

I spent a lot of months debating what to do with this Go & See study. After I taught it in November of 2017, the writing seemed half-finished and the task of making my lecture notes into something that I would be proud of or happy to share with others too daunting. I could imagine myself teaching it again, but putting it into actual chapters that someone could read and work through on her own—that took the Spirit a little longer to convince me I could do. And more important, it took me a while to believe for myself that putting this together was needed by others, delightful to the Lord, and worth the work and the risk.

I think it is just so dear of God to take my own teaching and require me to put it to practice with my writing. Perhaps that is what he was doing all along, trying to get me to see that I have a "talent" (Matthew 25:14–30) he wants to use right now. Just like many others, I often struggle to believe that he is really asking me to write. I struggle to believe that what I have is worth sharing. I struggle to believe that the outcome is in his hands and that my obedience is enough.

Throughout the years it has taken me to revise, edit, and format what you have in your hands, I was reminded over and over again that I am to persevere in helping others uncover their God-given gifts so that we can all keep building one another up, cheering one another on, and ushering in the kingdom of heaven through the body of Christ. I think this study is what that looks like for me. I say I think because I don't enter into this with great confidence in what this study will do for you but deeply aware that that's actually none of my business. God's got that taken care of. I am called to obey, use my gifts, take leaps of faith, and trust that he will deliver outcomes that work for the good as determined by his point of view.

I can tell you from firsthand experience that investing one's talents is sometimes exhausting. But hope reminds me that the rewards coming at the end of the race will be worth it. I really have no idea how God will use this experience for you. But my prayer is that it will stir you up toward love and good deeds. That it will uncover your eyes to the sovereignty and majesty of God in your life. And that when you are done you will view differently the gifts and talents you have been given—with more passion, excitement, and determination to put yourself in places that make God's miracle of multiplication necessary for your nourishment.

Thank you for sacrificing time and resources to embark on this Go & See journey. One of the greatest gifts we can offer one another is presence, and yours throughout this study is invaluable. I am excited to see what God does in all of us as we, together, let go of everything that hinders, fix our eyes on Jesus, and dig into understanding the course marked out just for us.

Your sister in Christ,
Jaclyn M. Loween

About This Study

I love stories. I teach language arts and communication, so it is no wonder that I like stories, and I absolutely love to teach students how to write so that they can express their thoughts, stories, and questions with confidence and accuracy. The gift of the desire to be a teacher began in me when I was in fourth grade. The details of God revealing to me that I would be a teacher someday are a bit fuzzy, but I distinctly remember that it was that year that I determined, "When I grow up, I want to be a teacher." And I never changed my mind.

It was a bit of a journey to see what subject area and age of students I would be best suited to teach. After exploring health and physical education, and even dietetics education, I circled back to language arts because learning to analyze literature and gaining skills in writing out my thoughts was also how I learned about myself, the world around me, and God. My English classes taught me about life, and I wanted to see God use me to reach into students' hearts and minds with literature and writing as a vehicle, not an end but a means. I believed that lives could be transformed by words because mine had been. And because I loved the fact that to teach literature was to also teach about the Word, the greatest story of all, written over thousands of years, kept intact only through a thousand miracles and the relentlessness of God's people to preserve it—the Bible. And in teaching writing, I would be able to give students the skills to record their life stories—their testimonies. Aren't these two—the Bible and our testimony—the most valuable things we have? And I would get to help students understand both!

Nothing is as powerful in one's life as knowing one's own story and seeing in it the truths, promises, and faithfulness of God recorded in the Bible. Others' stories are inspiring, but knowing your own story—truly picking it up and examining it and writing it down—has the power to change your life. Inspiring stories of others fail to do what your own story can, because when you read about another person's overcoming or success, it is all too easy to assume you are not able to do the same in your own life.

But when you nestle in close with Jesus, observe all that he has done in your life, and let him reveal to you how he has been writing a beautiful narrative out of your life all along, I am convinced you will be compelled to think and live differently because you will see yourself as one who is woven into the greatest story: the gospel. And in that revelation, you will find the perspective and courage to live out of the unique design God has created in you through the experiences he has given you in life, the natural talents, skills, and passions he set in your DNA, and through the relationships he has allowed you to participate in throughout the days you have been journeying this earth.

To that end, you will not find a lot of my story in this study. Not including my story or stories of others goes against traditional writing practices. I know this. However, I am going against the grain in this study because I want you to fully focus on your story. I wanted to remove stumbling blocks that would cause you to compare your story to another person's story, because this study is about you knowing who you are made to be in light of your design, not compared to others. This journey you are embarking on is full of reflection and digging deeply into the voice of God and his hand in your life. Choose to set aside comparisons or preconceived notions about who you think you are supposed to be based on other people's opinions of who you are or where you have come from. Instead, let the Holy Spirit, the insight of the Lord, and the intentional design of God's creation of you be your guidepost and point of reference.

One more drawback of not inserting many of my personal stories into this study is that it makes the study read a bit more like a textbook or a manual than a novel. But my mission is not to entertain. Rather, it is to instruct, encourage, and inspire. So to help you not get bogged down and bored, I have broken each lesson into six sections. This is to encourage you to take a mental break between sections and reflect on your story or the Bible.

You can work through each lesson at any pace you like. You could sit down for a few hours one day each week to work through an entire lesson in one sitting. Or you could do one lesson section each day of the week. Note, however, that "Tool" and "Next Step" sections will be more time-consuming than the other sections. So you'll want to plan a longer time to work on those days than on other days.

This study is not easy. It will require a lot of action via reflection and writing on your part. But if you are anything like me, that's where the rewards are to be found. It's the things that I have worked hardest at in life that have brought me closer to Jesus, increased my confidence in who he has made me to be, and stabilized my faith. As a sister and friend, I want to challenge you to persevere through all eight lessons, even if it takes you six months. I intentionally left off weeks and days in the formatting of the books so that you would not become discouraged if you didn't complete a lesson in one week. As a teacher, I am trained to observe the ways each student learns differently and then adapt expectations and assignment outcomes (and sometimes even deadlines) to honor those differences. I created the book in this way so that you too would not feel pressured to learn at the same pace as someone else—allowing you the freedom to spend more or less time on a section than someone else and truly let God be your guide through it all.

In your hands, you hold a toolbox. I believe God is going to ask each of you to use the tools here in different ways to see and accomplish different things. Will you strap on trust and endurance, faith and discipline, and joy and determination so that you can be motivated to invest what you have been given for such a time as this?

I pray that as you courageously *Go & See* what you have been given, your soul will experience a wrestling and a peace you've not known before, that your heart will beat strong rhythms of grace, and that your strength will be like that of Joshua, Daniel, Esther, and Deborah—heroes of the faith who knew who they belonged to, knew what they were called to do for God and others, and moved forward even when the world was at war around them. The same God who used these men and women to save his people lives in you. The same voice of God who called out to them to take action based on their unique design calls out to you too. I pray that the tools of this study will help you *Go & See* his good and perfect plan for the days he has numbered just right for you. He loves you. He has greatness built into you.

Go & See.

What Do You Have? Go and See.

Imagine a summer wind is brushing your hair back, and the gentle rock of the boat is calming your nerves because you know where you are going. For days you've been traveling, serving, and soaking in the Savior's instruction. Exhausted, your body, mind, and soul are ready to rest.

Let yourself settle into imagining these emotions being present in Jesus's disciples as they head across the lake, to the quiet place, in Mark 6:30–32. Moments earlier, Jesus had looked at their posture and recognized their exhaustion and hunger. Imagine a deep compassion in his voice as he says to them, "Come with me by yourselves to a quiet place and get some rest" (Mark 6:31).

Oh, dear one, can you relate to these disciples and their exhaustion and hunger?

Can you imagine yourself in need of the invitation to exit the busy and be alone with Jesus in a quiet place?

"Go get the boat, and head over to the other side of the lake; I will meet you there." Do you long for these words to be extended to you?

What if I told you they are?

He sees you! He sees your neediness. He invites you away. And you're almost there, to the quiet place of rest with Jesus.

This is the invitation of Go & See, to get away from all that keeps your mind and body busy in the day-to-day and see what Jesus has for you on the other side of the lake, in the quiet place. Here is the thing, though: what it looks like to find rest and nourishment with Christ just might go against the ideas you have in mind. It might actually look more like work than rest and may even feel like a burden at times. Jesus might answer your need with a need, a question, or unexpected expectations that might test your trust, faith, and will.

Believe and trust that he knows exactly what he is doing. He knows what you need to *see*. He knows where you need to *go*. He knows whose needs you'll be asked to meet. He is at your side, waiting to perform miracles with what you look for, discover, and bring back to show him.

In your hands, you hold a gift punched out by the tips of my fingers but crafted by the creator's work in my experiences, mind, and soul. I am a simple vessel setting before you and Christ what I have found. I pray that, as you work at unpacking it, God will multiply your strength, feed your soul, and refresh your understanding.

Thank you for accepting the invitation to *Go & See* what you have by stepping into the boat with me. It's time to head across the lake and find all that Jesus knows we need.

Lesson:1

Stones of Remembrance and the Call to Remember

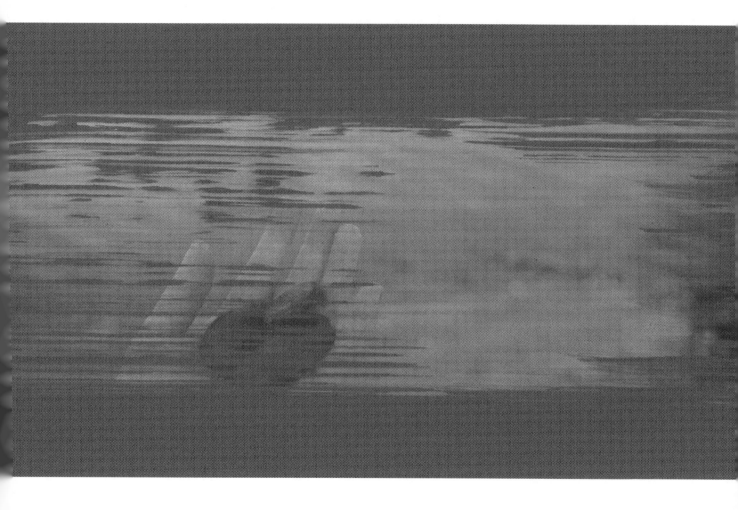

Go & See

Purpose and Context

God desires for us to Go & See how what we have can meet the needs of the "multitudes" when he miraculously multiplies the little bit we have.
Mark 6:30-44

We have all been given talents that we are asked to invest [multiply] until the day our master returns and asks us to give an account for what we did with what he gave us.
Matthew 25:14-30

We are forgetful. Thus, we need to set-up "stones of remembrance" as markers of God's faithfulness, strength and involvement in our journey.
Joshua 4

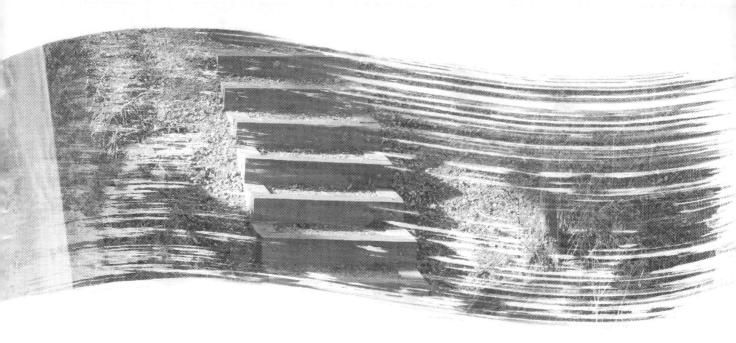

Introduction

We are all called to run the race of faith, one step at a time, inching toward heaven and wholeness. Our paces are different, our strategies unique and our strides timed to varying rhythms. There is a race marked out for you, but in order to *see* that more clearly, you may first need to step into discovering how your life's story is revealing who you are, who you are called to minister to, and how you are designed to do so with joy, purpose, and vision.

As you begin this journey, know that it is essential to invite the Holy Spirit into each step. He is the guide who holds the lamp lighting your way to knowledge, understanding, and wisdom. Second, you will need to set aside your doubts and insecurities and pick up the belt of truth, the breastplate of righteousness, the shield of faith, the helmet of salvation, and the sword of the Spirit (Ephesians 6:14–18).

Why?

Because throughout this study, you will need to remind your mind and soul to trust that your work is not in vain and that your heavenly Father delights in watching you seek to know and understand the gifts he has given you for such a time as this.

Let another truth penetrate your processing as well: your story is a part of the grand story of the gospel. Because of Christ's redemptive action on the cross, your testimony has a common denominator with every member of the church (past, present, and future). In this, we are one. Yet we know, love, and serve a God who is also intimately and specifically involved in each believer's life through the Holy Spirit. Let this inspire you to *see* your gifts, purpose, vision, and values as both a blessing to your life and the collective work of the church.

Finally, the gifts and purpose we are given are designed to equip us to love God fiercely and others extraordinarily. We need God. We need people. People need us. We were created

God desires for us to *Go & See* how what we have can meet the needs of the "multitudes" when he miraculously multiplies the little bit we have. **Mark 6:30-44**

by the relationship of the Trinity for a relationship with God and others. Christ's footsteps on earth became our salvation because God knew we needed to *see* with our eyes that relationship heals, relationship restores, relationship instructs, and relationship spurs all of us toward love and good deeds. To navigate this search to understand our gifts and purpose without taking account of and honoring the relationships that shape us would be to make only half the journey. Additionally, to arrive at knowing the unique combination of talents given to us without planning how to use them to invest in relationships with others would leave our souls only half satisfied and our human nature prone to using what we have for our own gain.

As you embark today, commit to *seeing* this study through, from start to finish. Admit that it will be challenging but that in Christ all things are possible. Most of all, though, enjoy the digging in. Revel in the *going*. Relish the *seeing*. Embrace the frustrations you may experience in remembering. In those moments, look up to heaven and believe God *sees* you and is cheering you on. He already knows what he has given you. His heart hurts for the ways the fallenness of the world has discouraged you or held you back. But he also knows that Christ's power in you is greater than the chains that want to bind you. Believe and claim the promise that you will find exactly what you need when you need it because God's sovereignty rules over the universe and the minor details of your life.

Three Bible passages provide the context and purpose of *Go & See*: Mark 6, Matthew 25, and Joshua 4. The bullet points below are a snapshot of how each passage will guide your journey and focus throughout the time you spend learning to use the tools provided in this study. My prayer is that this process will bring you joy, understanding, and confidence to propel you to live out the purposes you have been set on this earth to fulfill because you are you and you are here.

- ❏ God desires for us to *Go & See* how what we have can meet the needs of the "multitudes" when He miraculously multiplies the little bit we have (Mark 6:30–44).
- ❏ We have all been given talents that we are asked to invest (multiply) until the day our master returns and asks us to give an account of what we did with what he gave us (Matthew 25:14–30).
- ❏ We are a forgetful people. Thus, we need to set-up "stones of remembrance" as markers of God's faithfulness, strength, and involvement in our journey (Joshua 4).

Reflection & Application

Before we dig in, pull out your journal and get to a quiet place of mind. Below are some questions to get you thinking about what is ahead. In the education world, we call this accessing prior knowledge in order to spark learner interest. That is the aim. So answer the questions as fully as possible with whatever comes to mind. Check them off as you complete each one.

- ❑ **1)** What do you imagine when you hear the verse, "Come with me by yourselves to a quiet place and get some rest" (Mark 6:31)? Describe the expectations you would have of Jesus if you were told this by him:
    - ❑ **a)** Where is he taking you?
    - ❑ **b)** What will happen while you are there?
    - ❑ **c)** What will the outcome be of your time away with him?
- ❑ **2)** How can meeting the needs of others bring refreshing and rest?
    - ❑ **a)** Is there a time in your life where you were witness to this happening?
- ❑ **3)** Make a list of the natural and/or spiritual "talents" you are already aware you have.
    - ❑ **a)** In what ways are you working on multiplying one or more of your natural talents and/or spiritual gifts?
    - ❑ **b)** Is there a danger in not taking the time to *Go & See* what your natural talents and/or spiritual gifts are? Why or why not?
- ❑ **4)** How could the endeavor to remember the ways God has worked in your life help propel you forward from where you are right now?

Notes:

Notes:

_____

_____

_____

_____

_____

_____

_____

_____

_____

_____

_____

_____

_____

_____

_____

_____

_____

_____

Digging Deeper

First, take a few minutes to *go* and read Mark 6:30–44. Did you *see* the following?

- The disciples were exhausted from teaching and ministry.
- Jesus says, "Come with me by yourselves to a quiet place and get some rest." But the crowd found them there. (*Jesus knew this would happen. He sent them anyway.*)
- A need for a meal arises. The disciples want Jesus to send the people (and their needs) away.
- Jesus says, "You give them something to eat" (v. 37).
- Remember, they are already exhausted and thought they were heading to solitude with Jesus, not meeting a crowd of people to feed. (*How would you feel in these circumstances?*)
- After the disciples make excuses for how and why they can't feed the people, Jesus simply says, **"But what do you have? Go and see"** (paraphrasing v. 38).
- Jesus restores his disciples and nourishes the multitude by performing a miracle with the loaves and fish the disciples found when they *went* to *see* what they had.
  - We **see** in this story that Jesus doesn't meet needs and restore his people in a way we typically think of as the method we want God to use to meet our needs.
  - We **see** in this story that effort was required of the disciples to go and see what was there already.
  - We **see** also that the disciples humbly handing over to Jesus small and inadequate amounts of fish and bread resulted in the miracle of multiplication that met the needs of the multitude and the disciples. (With leftovers to boot!)

Next, take a few minutes to *go* and read Matthew 25:14–30. Did you *see* the following?

- To one he gave five talents, to another two and to another one, "each according to his ability" (v. 15).
- The men who received the five and the two talents "went at once" to increase what each had been given.
- The man with the one lived in fear and buried his talent, perhaps fearing he wasn't good enough or important enough to be able to increase his talent.
- The men who went and invested their talents believed, trusted, and obeyed their master—their actions were driven by their right understanding of their master's request and faithfulness.
- The man who hid his talent clearly had a misunderstanding of the master's heart and character: he distrusted the master and then blamed the master for his own inaction (vs. 24–25).
- The words of the master to the servant who chose not to invest his time in multiplying his talents are unsettling: **"Throw that worthless servant outside, into the**

darkness, where there will be weeping and gnashing of teeth" (Matthew 25:30).

- o He didn't commit any sins in regard to the Ten Commandments. He just didn't multiply his talent.
- o Does this startle you?

Finally, *go* and read Joshua 4. Pay close attention to the purpose and meaning of the "stones of remembrance" the men are **commanded** to set-up. Did you *see* the following?

- Joshua is leading this nation of God's chosen people out of a season of living in the desert into the Promised Land. In front of their eyes, the river Jordan quits flowing so they can cross.
- Pause and imagine the emotions and thoughts present in the hearts and minds of these people.
- After the successful crossing, God commands that Joshua instruct twelve men to each pick up a large stone from the Jordan and erect a monument out of them, as a memorial so that the future generations will know what God did that day.
- These stones are also to be set in place to signal that God stopped the Jordan, just as he had parted the Red Sea, "so that all the peoples of the earth may know that the hand of the Lord is mighty, that you may fear the Lord your God forever" (Joshua 4:24).

We are forgetful. Thus, we need to set up "stones of remembrance" as markers of God's faithfulness, strength and involvement in our journey.
Joshua 4

Images and instructions drawn from these three passages pin together the crux of the study ahead. The passage from Matthew shows us that God has talents for each of us, and we are commanded to multiply them until his return. The consequence of not doing so, though left to our imagination in the parable, is clearly costly and negative.

Jesus's interaction with the disciples in Mark reveals that rest and refreshing may not come in the package we want (spa day at the seaside, please!). But in the end, after the *going*, the *seeing*, and the blessing, the crowd is fed, the disciples get to participate in a miracle, and both physical and spiritual nourishment are bestowed upon them. In addition, the interruption of the crowd suggests that refueling may require us to exit the quiet place, face the needs of the multitude, and hear Jesus ask, "What are you going to do about this?" Which may be followed by some excuses that prompt Jesus to patiently ask again, "What do you have?"

The third passage is where we will end today—focusing on the story and image of stones found in Joshua, showing us that remembering is essential to remaining faithful. We are all prone to forgetfulness. The Old Testament makes that quite obvious. Thus, we start with remembering because most of the time we lose sight of what we have been given simply because we have forgotten to look back. We too quickly forget the ways God's faithfulness, his love, his pursuit of us, and his promises at work in our lives have shown up in our relationships, circumstances, vocations, and locations. To remember is to *Go & See* with fresh eyes God's gift of grace and redemption over our lives.

 ## Tool 1: Stones of Remembrance Timeline

Stones of Remembrance Timeline: The call to remember. The aim of this activity is for you to place on a timeline the "stones of remembrance" that testify to God's presence and work in your life. Imagine that each dot is a stone lifted up from a river and carried across to be set in place as a memorial, "so that all the peoples of the earth may know that the hand of the Lord is mighty, that you may fear the Lord your God forever" (Joshua 4:24 ESV).

As we have noticed in Joshua 4, God was present and evident in their time of need, despair, and doubt. So, don't forget to place on your timeline those experiences in your life that aren't all that pretty yet are testaments of hope, grace, truth, and deliverance.

In contrast, there are moments in life of pure joy, excitement, and accomplishment that also yell loudly of the Lord's presence and persistence in loving and pursuing us. So include those too.

In addition, our experiences are not the only testimony of God's involvement in our lives. People and places can mold our hearts and souls. Including significant people and places on your timeline will also help trigger your memory of God's providence and provision.

 ## Instructions

1. Take 5–10 minutes to pray, asking God to reveal to you the memories that you need to recall in order to *see* how your story reveals God's provision and plan to lead you to experiences, people, and places that built your understanding of your gifts (talents to invest) and purpose.
    a. Pray for remembrance, clarity, vision, and God's voice.
    b. Pray for strength, perseverance, and expectation.
    c. Pray for protection, peace, and efficiency.
2. Take a few minutes to journal or simply reflect on people, places, and experiences that make up the larger "stones" of your life's story—especially the ones that come to mind first.
3. Then take out a large piece of paper (*or use the timeline template included at the close of this lesson*), draw a long line down the middle, and begin creating a timeline of your life by plotting on the line a sequence of people, places, and experiences of your life.

a. Each memory, person, or place is a **stone** of remembrance.

b. Your timeline slots should be proportional to your memories, not necessarily your years of life.

c. Begin by writing down all the memories that come to mind. At this point, don't try to figure out the most important or applicable events of your life. Just write down *everything* you think of without trying to judge its importance or significance.

4. After placing as many "stones" as you can think of right now on the timeline, *Go & See* how your line is beginning to reveal clues to how your story is a monument to God's faithfulness, provision, and sovereignty.

5. Pause. Pray over the "stones" you have set up. Ask the Holy Spirit to help you *see*:

a. patterns that point to giftings,

b. answered prayers that point to faithfulness, and

c. suffering that points to provision.

The Next Step

Each day, for one week, choose to remember the details of one stone on your timeline by writing in your journal about it. Write as if you are sharing the memory with a friend to help them see God's hand in your story. Try to stick to the event as much as possible, without getting too wrapped up in the history of all that came before it. (But don't feel constrained; this is just a suggestion.)

Don't worry about grammar, spelling, punctuation, none of that! Just worry about getting your ideas down in a somewhat organized manner that could be used to communicate how your story reveals God's promises (*i.e., God's faithfulness, provision, sovereignty, redemption, grace, nearness, and so on.*). Remember, the stones the men were asked to pick up in Joshua 4 were heavy. Setting up the monument certainly took hard work, thoughtfulness, and time.

After completing each story, try to label it with a word or phrase that signifies the theme or message that the story carries about who God is. Then *see* if you can locate a verse or Bible passage that reveals the same theme, and write the scripture reference near that stone on your timeline. For example:

❑ **Theme**: God is faithful.
  ❑ **Verse**: If we are faithless, he remains faithful, for he cannot disown himself (2 Timothy 2:13).
❑ **Theme**: God sees me.
  ❑ **Verse**: The Lord looks down from heaven; he sees all the children of man (Psalm 33:13 ESV).

- ❏ **Theme**: God provides.
  - ❏ **Verse**: The Lord is my Shepherd; I lack nothing (Psalm 23:1).
- ❏ **Theme**: God is my rock.
  - ❏ **Verse**: The Lord is my rock, my fortress and my deliverer; my God is my rock, in whom I take refuge, my shield and the horn of my salvation, my stronghold (Psalm 18:2).
- ❏ **Theme**: God meets my needs.
  - ❏ **Verse**: My God will meet all your needs according to the riches of his glory in Christ Jesus (Philippians 4:19).

When you feel stuck or lacking in endurance, remember that you are doing this out of obedience and in order that you can *see* and share with others the testimony of God on this earth. He is with you in this process. His Holy Spirit is your source of inspiration. And Jesus delights in watching you use your gifts of intellect and words to pursue understanding, clarity, and awe.

Timeline

Timeline

Closing

The book of Proverbs is filled with gems of insight. Sometimes reading too many of them in a row overwhelms me. But I came across this one recently that set my heart ablaze because it spoke to something deep inside. "It is the glory of God to conceal a matter; to search out a matter is the glory of kings" (Proverbs 25:2).

I am a seeker-leaner by nature. I absolutely love to dig deep into certain topics or find the "proof" of an idea's accuracy. On the Myers-Briggs personality assessment, I score 75 percent in the Judging versus Perceiving category. Which basically means, I don't take things as they are. Before I make a decision I probe the available information until I believe I have all the "right" information.

This makes me a little nerdy, and sometimes I come across as a know-it-all in certain areas because I am prone to spouting research. (Only because I assume others also want to know *all* the information before they decide what they are going to believe about the topic.) This has landed me in a place of being scrutinized and misunderstood—tempting me to believe the lie that somehow I was wired wrong for ministry and that I don't fit outside the academic world. (Inside the academic world I feel at home!)

We have all been given talents that we are asked to invest [multiply] until the day our master returns and asks us to give an account for what we did with what he gave us.
Matthew 25:14-30

But do you know what this verse told me? It told me that the pleasure I find in seeking and searching glorifies God. Have you ever had someone say something so encouraging to you that it caught you off guard, and little sprinkles dropped into the corner of your eyes?

That is what this verse was to me. It revealed to me that how I am designed and what I enjoy were gifted to me on purpose for the glory of God and my own delight. It also told me that the "concealing of things" is by design and purpose—perhaps so that you and I can have the joy and pleasure of searching them out.

Someone once said, "The Bible reads you." This was true of me on that day (and other days too). And because it was right there in the Bible, I can now confidently affirm that I believe that God made me as a searcher to equip me for the ministry I am called to now. I needed to believe that about this part of me so that I could move forward unhindered by my own judgments of myself.

As you journey through this study, I pray that the process and the verses of the Bible will bring you to *see* that your unique design is needed in the church, necessary for the faith of others, and precisely set in place for such a time as this. As you *Go & See* what you have been given, be bold and brave. Ask the Lord to show you the "concealed" things intended for your discovery through remembering.

Lesson: 2

Incorporating Themes and Plotline Into Your Experiences

Purpose and Context

God desires for us to Go & See how what we have can meet the needs of the "multitudes" when he miraculously multiplies the little bit we have.

Mark 6:30-44

We have all been given talents that we are asked to invest [multiply] until the day our master returns and asks us to give an account for what we did with what he gave us.

Matthew 25:14-30

We are forgetful. Thus, we need to set-up "stones of remembrance" as markers of God's faithfulness, strength and involvement in our journey.

Joshua 4

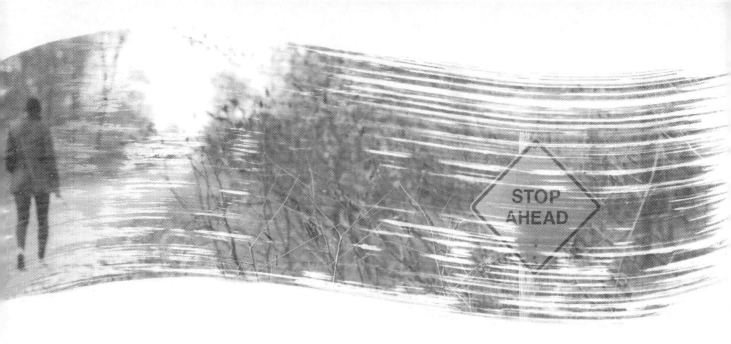

Introduction

First, if you are coming here today having completed a long timeline of your life, setting down on paper "stones of remembrance" of people, places, and experiences that have shaped your life, I want to say, "Kudos!" That likely took a lot of prayer, emotion, and perseverance of mind.

I imagine it took just as much effort as was required of the twelve men in Joshua 4 who were commanded to "take up each of you a stone upon his shoulder." These large stones would then be set in place as a memorial of remembrance. So when future generations asked, "What do these stones mean?" they would be reminded, "The Lord your God dried up the waters of the Jordan for you until you passed over, as the Lord your God did to the Red Sea, which he dried up for us until we passed over, *so that all the peoples of the earth may know that the hand of the Lord is mighty, that you may fear the Lord your God forever*" (Joshua 4:23–24 ESV, italics added).

Who will *see* your "stones" and *see* God because of them?

We are forgetful. Thus, we need to set up "stones of remembrance" as markers of God's faithfulness, strength and involvement in our journey.
Joshua 4

 ## Reflection & Application

Remembering is hard work that requires intentionality and planning. Over and over again in the Bible, particularly in the Old Testament, we see that forgetfulness led to faithlessness, which often led to delayed fulfillment of promises. We can stumble into the same pattern in our lives if we don't make a habit of going back and reflecting on the past, so that we are able to see forward more clearly.

So let's pause and reflect for a bit. Pull out your journal and get to a quiet place of mind. Then answer each question as fully as possible. Check off each one as you *go*.

❑ **1)** How can taking the time to remember and record the **people, places,** and **experiences of your life** help you *see* that your life is made up of stories that testify to God's presence and work on the earth?

   ❑ **a)** Which **people, places,** or **experiences** first come to mind when you ponder the application of the above question to your own life?

❑ **2)** Do you believe that just as the stones set up in Joshua 4 were meant to show all the peoples of the earth that the hand of the Lord is mighty to save, your "stones" can be set up to do the same?

   ❑ **a)** How can you live out this belief in tangible ways?

❑ **3)** Your stones (stacked one on top of the other) are meant to display God's sovereignty, grace, and relentless love to others. Who (*person or category of people*) do you think most needs to bear witness to your "stones" right now?

   ❑ **a)** What is the greatest obstacle you think you will face in setting up and sharing your "stones" with the people you listed above?

Notes:

_____

_____

_____

_____

_____

_____

_____

_____

_____

_____

_____

_____

_____

_____

_____

_____

_____

_____

Notes:

Digging Deeper

I believe taking the time to remember and record the **people, places,** and **experiences of your life** helps you *see* that your life is made up of stories that testify to God's presence and work on this earth, as it is in heaven. I believe sharing snapshots of your faith journey with others will increase the faith of those who *see* or hear. I believe that you just might need some tools to help you get those "stones" set up and put in place in such a way that others can *see* (read) them. But the real power is in the truth that God's hand is on your life. Your work in this study is to bring that power into the light and make it real, intimate, and etched into memory.

Not long from now, upon seeing (reading about) the "stones" you have set up, your children or others will be asking, "What do those stones mean?" And you'll be able to answer them, with a testimony that says, "The hand of God is mighty to save. The love of God is sovereign. The life of being a chosen one is full of Hosanna[1] moments, and there is a God who restores and redeems every one of these moments for His good purposes."

Yet setting up those "stones" and sharing what they mean in light of heaven can be very, very hard.

Why?

There is a myriad of reasons, but I think these are the top three:

1. You may not take enough time to reflect on the ways the **people, places,** and **experiences in your life** have connections, themes, and clues to your unique purpose, design, and testimony to the world.
2. You may struggle to mold your experiences into narratives that demonstrate God's involvement in and authorship of your stories.
3. You may not be in the habit of sharing the work of God's hand in your life openly with others. (This could be due to fear or because you just don't know how to work your testimony into everyday conversations.)

This lesson's tool is designed to help you jump over the hang-ups you might face in taking the "stones of remembrance" of your life and setting them up as a memorial for you and your people to be reminded of God's deliverance, faithfulness, and presence in your journey from here to heaven.

---

[1] "Help! Save me now!" Originally an appeal for deliverance (Heb. *hosia na*, "Please save"—Psalm 118:25), it came into liturgical usage to serve as an expression of joy and praise for deliverance granted or anticipated.

Tool 2: Thematic Labeling of "Stones"

Thematic Labeling of Stones: Giving a thematic organizational structure to the events of your life. The Bible sets up for us a story-line pattern that is used in nearly every book or movie that leaves the reader or viewer feeling satisfied at the end. (Do you find this a coincidence? I don't!)

Did you know that all good stories have these necessary components: characters, exposition, rising action, conflict, turning point (climax), and resolution? In literary analysis, scholars call this a plotline and use it to diagram and discuss the effectiveness of the various elements of a story. Likewise, authors use the plotline to organize the events of their stories throughout the writing process.

Below, you will see that the original plotline for a good story also runs through the story of the Bible, a story that continues on in your life and mine. No matter the testimony you have, it is a *good* story—it holds all the key components. Learning how to frame the events of your life in this way can help you connect your story to the plotline of the gospel, giving you unique and effective ways to share the gospel message with others.

Note the correlation between the elements of the plotline and the gospel story of the Bible as described below and shown in the images on the following page.

Essential Parts of a Story + Correlation to the Gospel Story

1. Exposition and Rising Action [**Creation**]: an introduction to the setting, character(s) and plot.
2. Conflict [**Fall]:** a struggle experienced by the character(s).
3. Turning point/Climax [**Redemption**]: a moment of redemption in which the character(s) or circumstances come to a change that moves the story toward a resolution.
4. Falling Action [**Life on Earth**]: everything that happens after the redemption moment that leads the character(s) and circumstances to a final, pleasing resolution.
5. Resolution [**Restoration – Heaven**]: the conflict is solved and the characters are restored and able to have peace.

It can be helpful to categorize your experiences and memories into these themes for a few reasons. First, it begins to help you frame your story in light of the gospel. Second, it allows you to go into the Bible and find passages that relate to the theme of your story and its correspondence to truths from God's word. Third, it can help you shape what you are called to share with others in a way that is engaging and satisfying to the hearer. Fourth, when you view your testimony in this way, you can more easily *see* that there is a divine and holy Author writing a beautiful story out of your life.

Plotline of a Good Story

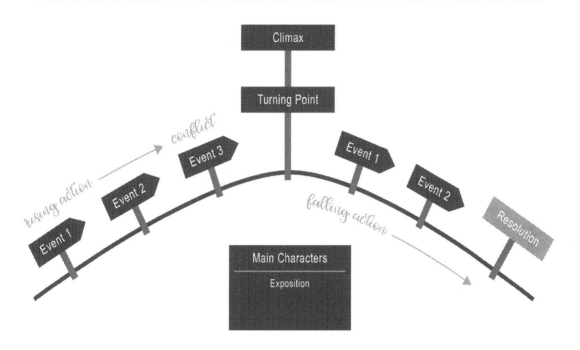

Correlation Between A Good Story & The Gospel

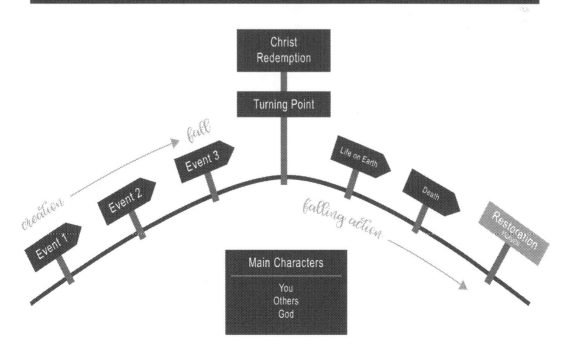

Instructions

After you have exhausted yourself with remembering (*via your stones of remembrance timeline from Lesson 1*), *Go & See* which themes (creation, fall, redemption, restoration) can be used to label the "stones" you have placed on your timeline. Try to categorize all "stones" with at least one of the themes, but not every experience you recall needs to have all four components. Use the following definitions to help you determine labels.

Creation: Times when something new was birthed, reborn or made new: education, marriages, jobs, children, dreams, visions ... → **Highlight these events/memories in yellow**.

Fall: Times when something was broken, torn away, damaged, or lost. This could be physical, emotional, or spiritual. Desert times. Hardships caused by the choices you made or circumstances around you. → **Highlight these events/memories in green.**

Redemption: Memories of times when you witnessed God bringing you (or someone else) to a turning point: Turning away from something that was distracting you from him. Turning from destructive behavior or thinking to wholeness and truth. Choosing "no" to lies or unhealthy habits. → **Highlight these events/memories in blue**.

Restoration: Memories of something in or around you being made new, healed, restored, or cleaned up. A relationship mended. A vision restored. A dream coming to fruition. A physical or emotional wound being healed. → **Highlight these events/memories in pink**.

Here are some tips to help you with getting your ideas out of your head and onto paper:

- Before labeling the "stones" on your timeline, next to each, draw pictures or jot down just enough words to remind you about the details of the experience and the impact it had on you. (You will write out more details in Lesson 4.)
- When you feel stuck, stop and pray. Ask the Holy Spirit to reveal. Wait on him to show you what the big "stones" of your story are that need to be shared with the coming generation(s).
- Take time each day (FYI: morning is when your mind is freshest) to reflect and add details to your timeline and labels to the stones on it.

The Next Step

Connecting the **people, places,** and **experiences of your life** to truths and specific Bible verses can help deepen the experience of remembering and labeling the "stones" of your timeline. The retelling of your experiences and reflections of what you have learned from them are powerful and valuable. Yet when you can also weave the words of scripture in to support the themes or lessons you have learned, a "breath of life" is added, increasing the power and impact because you are allowing God's words to be present in your remembering, writing, and sharing.

So the next step to take after labeling all your stones is to find Bible passages that support the theme of what you now *see* God has revealed to you about himself or about you from the experiences on your timeline. To find specific scriptures or generalized biblical truths to incorporate when it comes time to write about or share your "stones" with others, you can use:

❑ your knowledge of the Bible (verses you have memorized),
❑ your Bible's topical concordance (if it has one), or
❑ an online topical Bible (for example, Biblegateway.com or Biblehub.com).

Then, either on a separate sheet of paper or next to each "stone" on your timeline, record the Bible verses you find that could be worked into the telling of your story. Down the road, this will help you convey the intended truth you desire your testimony to reveal.

Closing

I would like to close this session with a testimony to how this tool, along with the power of the Holy Spirit, set one woman free and empowered her to claim a promise from the Bible over her future.

A few weeks after teaching this series as a class to a small group of women, I received a note from an attendee. She had written,

> I did my timeline on a literal line from birth to the date of our class. When I finished my timeline, I looked at it and was prompted to subtract the years depression started (month and year) until class. It was exactly 40 years! Then I felt this strong sense of peace as I considered this observation, "You were in the desert for 40 years and now you're out!" Believe me, I am claiming that promise!

I close with this for two reasons: First, the tool is great, but the power is in the working of the Holy Spirit. Second, to show that remembering, writing, and creating a visual of your life

in this way has the potential to shift your perspective, help you see and claim promises of God, and move you forward into your calling and purpose.

As you work with this tool, invite the Holy Spirit into the process. Set aside quiet time to sit and look at what you have remembered. Allow your soul, mind, and heart to be open to hearing from the Lord messages intended just for you.

Go & See.

We are forgetful. Thus, we need to set up "stones of remembrance" as markers of God's faithfulness, strength and involvement in our journey.

Joshua 4

Lesson: 3

Fighting for a Clear-Conscience

Go & See

Purpose and Context

God desires for us to Go & See how what we have can meet the needs of the "multitudes" when he miraculously multiplies the little bit we have.

Mark 6:30-44

We have all been given talents that we are asked to invest [multiply] until the day our master returns and asks us to give an account for what we did with what he gave us.

Matthew 25:14-30

We are forgetful. Thus, we need to set-up "stones of remembrance" as markers of God's faithfulness, strength and involvement in our journey.

Joshua 4

Introduction

Because of God's grace and sovereignty, we get to choose *bravery* to *go* and *see* how, even out of painful experiences, we can be led to our greatest *purpose*. This may require some *wrestling* with hard questions and emotions, along with facing hindrances, but when we let the Holy Spirit in to clear our conscience, we can run our race with confidence.

I would like you to keep two overarching themes in mind as you journey through this lesson:

- Bravely wrestling with questions of yourself and your experiences is necessary and can produce a clear and strong conscience. Working forward from a place of clarity allows you to fix your eyes on Jesus and all that he has given you to equip you to live on a purposeful mission.
- The Holy Spirit's presence and power are what will lead you to revelation, peace, and instruction. Only through the supernatural strength and insight provided by Christ living in you, and his helper (the Holy Spirit), can you see beyond earthly realities to eternal perspectives and motives.

 ## Reflection & Application

By faith we are saved and washed with the blood Jesus poured out at the cross. Yet we are still prone to stumble and live in patterns of sin or lies that hold us back from fully living out God's purpose for our lives. It can be difficult to find time and space to open our hearts up in front of the Lord and ask him to *reveal, heal,* and *set free.* But all of these are essential to being able to *Go & See* what we have.

We best remember, write, and operate from a place of freedom. The alternative is to operate out of fear: fight, flight, or freeze, which literally blocks our brain from higher level thinking, learning, and making progress. In addition, to remember, write, and operate from a place

We have all been given talents that we are asked to invest [multiply] until the day our master returns and asks us to give an account for what we did with what he gave us.
Matthew 25:14-30

of freedom requires some reflective space and actions on our part. Consider the actions mentioned in the following verses and the instruction they provide for us:

- "Everyone who names the name of the Lord must *turn away* from unrighteousness … *Flee* from youthful passions, and *pursue* righteousness, faith, love and peace, along with those who call on the Lord from a pure heart" (2 Timothy 2:19, 22 ESV, italics added).
- We can be loosed from the patterns of sin and guilt in our lives through the conviction and power of the Holy Spirit, faith and the work of the cross. Second Corinthians 3:18 says, "We, who with unveiled faces, all reflect the Lord's glory, are *being transformed* into his likeness with ever-increasing glory, which *comes* from the Lord, who is the Spirit" (NIV 1984, italics added).
- "If anyone *purifies* himself from anything dishonorable, he will be a special instrument, *set apart*, *useful* to the Master, *prepared* for every good work" (2 Timothy 2:21 CSB, italics added).

The clearing of the conscience is a process. (*The priesthood consecration ceremonies took seven days!* If you're curious, *Go & See* Exodus 29 for evidence.) The conscience-clearing process begins with asking some hard questions of our hearts and souls and asking the Holy Spirit to come in as our teacher and guide. Settle into a quiet place with a journal, and write down your answers to the following questions:

- ❑ **1)** What are some patterns in your life that you know you need to be turning away from?
- ❑ **2)** Is there evidence in your life of pursuing righteousness, faith, love, and peace?
  - ❑ **a)** If not, what things are distracting you and taking up your time?
  - ❑ **b)** If yes, what evidences (fruit) reveal this to be true in your life?
- ❑ **3)** Are there dishonorable things you need to confess?
  - ❑ **a)** If yes, name them specifically and describe how you will turn from them.
  - ❑ **b)** If not, what actions, habits, or practices have helped you steer clear of dishonorable things you struggled with in your past?

Notes:

Notes:

As hard as it may be to bring another person into these areas of your life, summoning up the courage and strength to confess your failures and successes with a trustworthy friend can potentially lift heavy burdens from your heart and mind. Take a few minutes and just sit quietly with the Lord, asking him to reveal to you if you should share your reflections with someone. If you sense that he is asking you to do so, then ask him to reveal to you the right person to invite into this process to encourage you, hold you accountable, and partner in the battle with you.

 ## Digging Deeper

Knowing your God-given purpose and God's plans for you can be helpful in motivating you to persevere in living out of a faith rooted in a clear conscience. Ephesians is a marvelous book to study when trying to understand the purpose of the body of Christ and the command to the individuals of the body—namely, to share God's plan for the world, and to serve and love with power and unity of purpose and mind. For this lesson, let's *Go & See* the wisdom we can glean from Ephesians 3:7–11, as the apostle Paul encapsulates the purpose and vision set out for him by God. You will see his purpose is not that different than yours and mine.

> Of this gospel I was made a minister *according to* the gift of *God*'s grace, which was *given me by* the working of *his power.* To me, though I am the very least of all the saints, this grace *was given*, to preach to the Gentiles the unsearchable riches of Christ, and to bring to light for everyone what is the plan of the mystery hidden for ages in God, who created all things, *so that through the church* the manifold wisdom of God might now be made known to the rulers and authorities in the heavenly places. This was *according to the eternal purpose* that he has realized in Christ Jesus our Lord. (ESV, italics added)

Did you *see* the following?

- Our purpose and vision come to us as a *gift* of God's grace. Individually, we are equipped with the *power of grace* (the power that raised Christ from the dead) to share the gospel with others through the life we live—*so that through the church* God's glory, wisdom, *power,* and might are revealed to everyone on earth and the rulers and authorities in heaven.
- We have more than just an earthly purpose. The lives we live here as members of the church body have the purpose of witnessing God's majesty and reign to the heavenly realms too.
- The equipping to live our purpose is generated by the working power of God and was planned according to God's eternal purposes, set up before time.

- Paul recognizes his purpose is appointed. He doesn't generate it himself, nor does he aim to complete it in his own strength.
- We too have been appointed to reach particular people in our corner of the world. How we do that depends on our giftings and areas of influence, all of which are given to each of us through the grace of God.
- Our strength to live according to our eternal purpose was provided for each of us at the cross, where Christ died to redeem our every moment and enable us to serve faithfully in bringing to light, for everyone around us, the plan of God for redemption, reconciliation, and restoration.

Wow! Right?

Let's look at a couple more passages that demonstrate God's purpose being written into your story before it was even revealed to you or comprehensible to your soul. In 1 Corinthians 15:9–10, Paul again shows us that he did not determine his purpose himself. It was given to him by God. (*Go* and read it, and come right back.)

In verse 10 he states, "**By the grace of God I am what I am**." In other words, my past and my present are not outside God's hand of grace and purpose. So also for you! The scars or mishaps of your past don't cast you outside the calling and purpose to live out the gospel and share Christ with the people God places in your life. All who claim the name of Jesus as Lord and Savior have a divine appointing and anointing to do this because Christ's death on the cross made each of us members in the royal priesthood (1 Peter 2:9) and the indwelling Holy Spirit gives us the power to "do all things" (Philippians 4:13).

Let that sink in for a little bit. *Your life has a divine and holy purpose*, because it was written on your heart and soul before the beginning of time. Still, it isn't easy to *Go & See* how to use your gifts, time, talents, and experiences to live out your purpose for such a time as this.

Why is it that both *seeing* what you have and living out of your divine purpose is so hard?

First, because we live in a fallen world, and we have an enemy who likes to entangle us in snares, knock us off course, and steal the gifts we have been given to bring Jesus's name and saving grace to the lonely and hurting. In my life, and possibly in yours too, this wrestling match starts in my mind, making it hard to detect the attack.

Second, "I am a human, raised by humans" (the movie *Elf*). In this human condition I am prone to faults, failures, and sins that cloud my vision, inhibit my motives, and may even derail me from the path marked out for me. The human condition has its hold on all of us while we walk on this broken planet.

As a result, we have to *work at pursuing* and *maintaining* a clear conscience: persisting in not allowing faults, failures, and sins to impede us from faithfully, joyfully, and powerfully living a life that utilizes all the God-given gifts provided to us as a means for reaching the world around us.

In the book of 2 Timothy you will *see* that Paul teaches us that serving with a clear conscience comes from not taking credit for our accomplishments *or our failings*. In addition, we *see* that a clear conscience arises out of believing we have a divine calling and being equally convinced we did nothing to earn it. (*Go* and read the whole book of 2 Timothy. It will take you approximately eleven minutes. I timed it for you.)

Did you *see* in the verses of this chapter that we are also not powerful enough to ruin God's plans?

And we know that in all things God works for the good of those who love him, who have been called according to his purpose.
Romans 8:28

Admitting that even in what seems to be our time of greatest failure, he can make all things work for the good of those who love him and are called according to his purpose (Romans 8:28) requires faith, humility, and trust. To get to this place in our believing is to land in our sweet spot. Operating out of this sweet spot is our flourishing. We will never fully arrive at this place before heaven, but in Christ and through the Holy Spirit, we will experience it on the days we *need it*, when God "stoops down" and offers grace to us (Psalm 18:35). And on the days when we fight for it with all the "armor of God" provided to us to do battle (Ephesians 6:10–18).

Fighting for a clear conscience is doable and necessary for us to run with assurance and confidence the races marked out for us. Therefore, you need to take the time to sit with and reflect upon the past and present choices, actions, and thoughts of your life and mind in order to *Go & See* how your God-given gifts were intended for such a time as this.

To further explain and clarify, let's take a look at a passage in Hebrews 10:19-24. In this passage we see both how our conscience is set to cleanliness and the result of letting the Holy Spirit come in and clean house.

> Therefore, brothers and sisters, *since* we have confidence to enter the Most Holy Place *by the blood of Jesus*, by the new and living way opened for us through the curtain, that is, his [Jesus's] body, and *since* we have a great high priest over the house of God, let us *draw near to God* with a sincere heart in full assurance of faith, *having our hearts sprinkled* [by the blood shed at the cross] *to cleanse us from a guilty conscience* and having our bodies washed with pure water. Let us hold unswervingly to the hope [of our purpose and calling] we profess, for he who promised is faithful. And let us consider how we may spur one another on toward love and good deeds. (italics added)

These verses make it clear that we are already cleaned and given a clear conscience because of the atoning work of Jesus as the sacrificial lamb for all mankind. So, it isn't that we have to work to gain a clear conscience by doing this or that. It is that we have to work at *remembering, seeing, and admitting the ways we have fallen short, made choices out of fear or envy, participated in actions that harmed ourselves or others, or perhaps let doubt win over belief.* It is taking the time and space to let our hearts break for what breaks the heart of God and admit that maybe what breaks his heart hasn't been our priority.

It takes sitting in that grief long enough to feel the weight of the consequences of our sin. The point is not to feel shame or condemnation but to be able to feel, know, and understand all that we have been saved from. True humility, the kind that brings our souls and hearts to understanding deeply a right posture toward God, is found in *going* to some of those dark places of our hearts and minds, admitting that we *see* them and *then* choosing to believe that the light of truth, the power of the Spirit, and the cleansing power of Christ wash it all clean.

In an effort to pull in your sense of sight to this process of learning, set your pen down and examine closely the image below. You will see hands gently preparing for washing. Meditate on the verses from Ezekiel as you consider the message available in the details of the picture.

- "I will give them an undivided heart and put a new spirit in them; I will remove from them their heart of stone and give them a heart of flesh" (Ezekiel 11:19).
- "I will give you a new heart and put a new spirit in you; I will remove from you your heart of stone and give you a heart of flesh" (Ezekiel 36:26).

As you sit with this image for a minute or two, ask the Lord to reveal to you what parts of you are most in need of a washing of cleansing and renewal?

- ☐ Is it the ambition of your heart?
- ☐ Is it the thoughts of your mind?
- ☐ Is it the wounding of your heart?
- ☐ Is it the power of your strength?

From heaven, he is reaching down with the purest of waters, pouring over you rain that will both clean and fill—opening the doors for your words, actions, and life to be a cleansing stream from which others can receive peace, healing, and strength.

 ## Tool 3: Stone Washing

Stone Washing: A tactile learning experience. Research shows that we learn best when we experience the intended lesson with our five senses: touch, smell, taste, hearing, and sight. This activity is designed to allow you to engage in as many of those as you can, so that your brain can hold on to the memory and your heart can sense God's touch.

In addition, our ability to recall is increased when touch, smell, taste, hearing, or sight is associated with a memory. In particularly difficult memories, these senses can trigger negative emotions. But God is the great healer, and he wants to come into those broken and hard places of your heart's memory, establish clean memories, and replace sensory triggers. But it may require some courage and action on your part to invite the Holy Spirit into those places and build in your brain some new wiring systems to work with.

As you work through the steps of this activity, imagine that it is God's hands washing over the words on your stones. Imagine that he is taking rocky parts of your heart and turning those stones to flesh (Ezekiel 36:26). Get to a quiet place, and let him wash over your heart as you symbolically wash these memories. Ask God to replace the negative sensory details with the ones that are in front of you: warm water, fragrant soap, clean hands, and erased words. Let his grace come in and reveal to you all that needs revealing in order for you to have a clear conscience with which to run freely in your purpose and giftings.

Instructions

1. Gather the following items: 3–5 stones big enough to write at least one word on; a Sharpie marker; soapy, warm water; and scrub sponge.

2. Review your timeline (from Lessons 1 and 2) and the reflection questions from this lesson. Most of all, let yourself reflect on both the Fall and Redemption "stones" from your timeline or any events that are marked with painful memories. Take special care to reflect intently on those recalled moments that bring with them discouragement, doubt, or anger.

3. If you don't have any "stones" on your timeline that reflect suffering or falling away from nearness to God, then pause and pray, and wait a bit longer. Hard memories sometimes get suppressed; be willing to wait and keep asking for revelation. Then record any experiences that are revealed on your timeline or in your journal.

4. Next, take a stone for each memory that has come to mind that needs grace, perspective, or forgiveness.
   a. Choose one word to describe each moment or memory.
   b. Then write the words you have chosen down, one per stone.

5. Pause, pray.
   a. Ask God to usher in his grace and to give you divine understanding of the purpose and intention of those moments.
   b. Ask God to heal those moments, and envision your heart being sprinkled with Christ's atoning power and your soul being washed with pure water.
   c. Then ask the Holy Spirit to give you a clear conscience, free of guilt or condemnation and full of humility and grace-filled perspectives.

6. Once you have had time to reflect, listen, and feel God wrapping himself around your memories, take your stones and wash them clean in soapy water. Scrub them **until the words are gone**.

7. Next set a timer for ten minutes. Using the **Stone Washing Activity Reflection** page, draw or write out a reflection, prayer, poem, or song that reveals the thoughts, emotions, or understanding this activity generated in you.

8. Finally, set the stone(s) in a place where you will be able to see them as you do your homework for this week.

Stone Washing Activity Reflection

After you have completed the Stone Washing Activity in Lesson 3, take some time to reflect on your experience. Set a timer for ten minutes, and use that time to draw or write out a reflection, prayer, poem, or song that reveals the thoughts, emotions, or understanding this activity generated in you.

Freely write down all that comes to mind as you document this part of your journey. Or if it helps you focus, you could use the following prompt to guide your reflection: What do you want to remember from this experience?

Notes:

The Next Step

Another area to consider in the process of working toward operating out of a clear conscience is guilt, lies, and shame. We can genuinely repent, turn our backs on a sin, and seek forgiveness from people we hurt and still carry the terrible burden of guilt. Until we let Christ's work on the cross not only save our souls but cleanse our consciences, our own self-destructive tendencies may unwittingly team with the devil to bully us with bouts of mental torment (Beth Moore, *The Entrusted Study*). These often present themselves as lies we believe about ourselves or others.

Let's pause and reflect on this struggle of the mind for a bit. Pull out your journal and get to a quiet place of mind. Then answer each question as fully as possible. Check off each one as you go.

❑ **1)** Are there lies I am believing about my abilities, talents, gifts, or purpose?
    ❑ If yes, write out each lie. Claim truth over it. Cross out the lie. Then write out the truth next to it. If applicable, find a Bible verse that supports the truth, and write it down to memorize.
❑ **2)** Are lies controlling an area of my life or my identity?
    ❑ If yes, write out the lie. Claim truth over it. Cross out the lie. Then write out the truth next to it. If applicable, find a Bible verse that supports the truth, and write it down to memorize.
❑ **3)** Are there people I need to forgive in order to break the chains of these lies?
    ❑ If yes, write out any lies you are believing about each person. Claim truth and healing over your relationship with them. Cross out the lies. Write out the truth and a prayer asking for healing. If applicable, find a Bible verse that supports the truth, and write it down to memorize.

By periodically reflecting on questions like the ones above, we line up our sights to quickly target lies, guilt, and condemnation as schemes and snares designed to trip us up. No doubt about it, the fight we fight is not against flesh and blood but against the powers and principalities of the world (Ephesians 6:12). And the enemy's cleverness can sometimes almost knock us down by insisting to us that our battle is with the people around us.

But we can put on the armor of God when we see these lies beginning to settle in and fight with the weapons we have been given in Christ—truth, righteousness, faith, the gospel, salvation and the Spirit—and live as if we really believe the following is true of us: "We demolish arguments and every pretension that sets itself up against the knowledge of God, and we take captive every thought to make it obedient to Christ" (2 Corinthians 10:5).

There are things in our past we may always wrestle to overcome. Even Paul was not released from his "thorn in the flesh," and he was starting churches, discipling the next generation, and writing what would become much of the New Testament, all while being in prison. Upon his repeated requests to God to remove this struggle from his life, God answered, "No"—followed by "My grace is sufficient for you, for my power is made perfect in weakness" (2 Corinthians 12:9).

As you face beating down lies, guilt, and condemnation, or wrestle with suffering, don't get discouraged when the outcome doesn't come quickly or in the way you imagine it should. Your God is fighting for you, and he is also extending you power that is made perfect in weakness (Exodus 14:14; Deuteronomy 3:22; 2 Corinthians 12:9). Keep pressing on in battle, but don't forget to lean into Him and trust fully in His plans for you.

Closing

Exposing what isn't hidden anyway still has a way of summoning up fear and trepidation. The author of Hebrews clearly understood this because he opens Hebrews 10:19-24 with reminding us that we can draw near with the assurance provided to us through our faith, believing that laying before him all that has been trapping us in guilt has been overcome and cleansed. We need only to draw near, admit those things that are chaining us to guilt, and then believe the cleansing is in His hands, literally. The nails in his hands took that guilt for us so that we could hold unswervingly to the hope we profess, and experience a life without condemnation (Hebrews 10:23, Romans 8:1).

You and I, we have access to a "true heart" fully assured and confident because of our faith. Yet, the daily toil of life in this world can sometimes hold us back or trip us up. This is not new (*Consider some of the "heroes" of the Bible and the actions they took: Jacob, Noah, and David, to name a few.*). Nor is it surprising to God. Yet, if we don't let God come in and deal with the guilty conscience that has resulted from our failures or unbelief, we'll lack assurance, hemorrhage faith, and default to condemnation that could cripple our ability to *Go & See* how Christ has equipped us for His purpose and calling.

Our hearts are already "sprinkled" and our bodies "*washed*" by the atoning power of Christ, but we need to make sure we take the time to recognize exactly what poor choices he has redeemed, what broken relationships he has restored, and what condemning self-talk and lies he has set us free from. **The chains have been broken, but if we only see them locking up invisible, unnamed things, we will not fully realize all that he has done for us, and our conscience will not fully understand the clean-state in which we live.**

When we can see clearly what we have been set free from, our freedom will lead us to greater courage and strength to help others see their freedom too. Additionally, we will be keenly aware that using our freedom to set others free is our one mission no matter the location of our feet or the vocation of our hands. Don't quit *Going & Seeing* what God has done for you. Make remembering all that your conscience has been cleared from become a part of your regular reflections. It just might change everything about how you live your tomorrows.

Go & See.

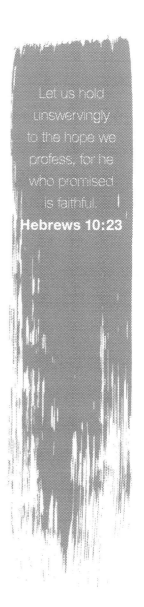

Let us hold unswervingly to the hope we profess, for he who promised is faithful.

Hebrews 10:23

Notes:

Notes:

Lesson: 4

Communicating a Larger Truth With Your Story

Go & See

Purpose and Context

God desires for us to Go & See how what we have can meet the needs of the "multitudes" when he miraculously multiplies the little bit we have.
Mark 6:30-44

We have all been given talents that we are asked to invest [multiply] until the day our master returns and asks us to give an account for what we did with what he gave us.
Matthew 25:14-30

We are forgetful. Thus, we need to set-up "stones of remembrance" as markers of God's faithfulness, strength and involvement in our journey.
Joshua 4

Introduction

Lesson 3, Fighting for a Clear Conscience, was a heavy undertaking, wasn't it? If you took the time to work through all components, or even most of the components, I hope you are able to see how brave, strong, and courageous you are.

In this lesson, you are going to go one step further in unpacking and understanding how, even out of painful experiences, we can be led to our eternal visions and purposes. The aim of the following is to give you tools to *Go & See* how a single life experience can show the redemptive power of Christ and give testimony to the work of God. This will be done by examining the instructions for writing a personal essay and then recording a memory from your timeline in a personal essay format.

This may seem more academic than spiritual, but I have found that separating the secular and the sacred is a man-made way of categorizing and that God never intended us to live believing that some activities are spiritual and others are not. When we choose a life lived in Christ, all that we put our hands and minds to is encompassed by the hands and presence of our Creator.

That said, as you step into the reading and activities for Lesson 4, don't let their academic nature limit your motivation to complete them. Don't let yourself believe that they are not spiritual enough to produce a powerful, communing experience between your soul and our God. The Spirit is our helper—enabling us to gain knowledge and find understanding. And he lives in you! Therefore, you have full access to knowledge and understanding through him. Ask for them to guide you as you reflect and write.

Many of the prompts and examples in this session relate to how reflecting on times of suffering, hardship, or trials holds immense power to lead us to understanding our purpose and using our gifts. In the midst of hardship we often fail to *see* the good impact these experiences are producing in our faith, growth, and destiny. However, that doesn't mean

You intended to harm me, but God intended it for good to accomplish what is now being done, the saving of many lives.

Genesis 50:20

God can't also use experiences of success, triumph, or joy to reveal our purpose and gifts. So as you determine what to focus on in your personal essay, feel free to pull any life experience into the light if it reveals God using your life experiences to help you *see* your identity and his character more clearly.

Reflection & Application

In the "Digging Deeper" portion of this lesson, we will be looking at some important lessons we can glean from the story of Joseph—the boy sold into slavery who was eventually placed in a position of leadership that equipped him to save the lives of many, including the brothers who sold him into slavery in the first place.

If we were to chart Joseph's suffering on a timeline, from the great dreams of his youth to the time he was put in charge of the land, we would likely see a span of thirty to forty years. That is a lot of years of wading through undesirable and undeserved circumstances. Yet Joseph chose to use his gifts no matter what was going on around him. And in the midst of it all, Joseph experienced the presence of God and the fulfillment of those early dreams.

In a world that honors comfort and seeks materialistic rewards as symbols of success, it is sometimes hard to believe God is sovereign in both the favor and suffering in our life. Let's pause and reflect on all of this for a bit. Pull out your journal and get to a quiet place of mind. Then answer each question as fully as possible. Check off each one as you *go*.

- ❑ **1)** When you look at your own life, are you able to *see* how both the favor and the suffering (disappointments, obstacles, pain) are in the hands of a God who loves you deeply? Explain why or why not.
- ❑ **2)** Has there been a time in your life (or the life of someone you know) when suffering resulted in others (outside of the circumstance) *seeing* God more clearly? Describe this experience and the impact it had.
- ❑ **3)** Have you felt the Lord's presence in times of suffering (disappointments, obstacles, pain)? Describe what those moments were like and how they have impacted your relationship with God.

Notes:

Notes:

Digging Deeper

Understanding doesn't often come in the midst of a trial or hardship. Even science reveals that the brain has a hard time learning when under stress, so it makes sense that it isn't until after the struggle has passed that we are able to cognitively and emotionally revisit challenging experiences of our lives and mine out the diamonds from the rough. The discoveries scientists have made in recent years while studying the brain and learning are also truths that we see in the stories of the men and women of the Bible. In addition, present-day Bible teachers like Beth Moore and Jennie Allen point out the following in regard to the relationship between understanding suffering in light of purpose and calling. Note the two examples below:

- Many of us have walked onto the path of our divine calling with a wounding. Perhaps it's time we quit thinking that it's an accident (Beth Moore, *Entrusted*).
- Out of our pain, we could heal the world (Jennie Allen, *Restless*).

Yet, most important to our journey is to *Go* to the source of all truth, the Bible, where the words are sharper than a two-edged sword (Hebrews 4:12) and are designed to instruct us on how to navigate life in this fallen world in a way that is in line with our divine purposes, talents, and gifts.

Take a few minutes to *Go* and read what is written in these passages: Philippians 3:10; James 1:2–4; 1 Peter 4:12–13; Genesis 50:20; 2 Corinthians 1:3–7; John 15:18–19; and 2 Timothy 1:12.

Did you *see* the following?

- Jesus is best known through suffering (Philippians 3:10).
- We get stronger through suffering (James 1:2–4).
- Suffering on earth can cause us to long for heaven (1 Peter 4:12–13).
- Even the darkest moments of your life God is able to use for your good and the good of others. Our lives will leave a mark on history because of the testimony God builds into our stories of trial (Genesis 50:20).
- Out of our suffering, we find comfort to bring comfort to others (2 Corinthians 1:3–7).
- Servants of Jesus suffer some things in direct correlation to the positions God calls them to fill (John 15:18–19; 2 Timothy 1:12).

These verses suggest, also, that a measure of our pain and hardship really is connected to the purpose of our calling. Some of it is spiritual warfare. Some of it is sociological resistance because the world hates us as it hated Jesus. Some of it's ordained by God for our growth, our humility, our compassion, our obedience, our completion, our faith, and our future crown, joy, and fellowship in His glory. If we refuse to partake in the sufferings of Christ, we will miss partaking in the explosive joy that comes in the overcoming. And as Beth Moore writes in her study, *Entrusted*, "Sometimes hardships will come because you got it right."

Next, let's take a deeper look into the story of Joseph. Joseph's testimony is one of my favorites because his life reveals so purely how purpose and vision can sometimes take years and suffering in order to be fulfilled at just the right time. This gives me hope, peace, and trust in the moments when I doubt whether my feet are planted in the "right" places. Joseph's faithfulness, in the times when it seemed the circumstances didn't promote his designed purpose, has frequently helped me dismiss circumstances as the voice to understanding my gifts, purpose, and vision.

Go & See what is recorded in Genesis 37:12–36 and 39:1–23, and highlight the verses that stick out to you. Then come back and take note of the following:

- "But while Joseph was there in the prison, the Lord was with him; he showed him kindness and granted him favor in the eyes of the prison warden. So the warden put Joseph in charge of all those held in the prison, and he was made responsible for all that was done there. The warden paid no attention to anything under Joseph's care because the Lord was with Joseph and gave him success in whatever he did" (39:20–23).
- When given the opportunity to turn his back on God and escape circumstances, Joseph remained faithful to his post.
- We see in Joseph's story that God was in control of Joseph's favor and in control of Joseph's suffering.
- People who crossed Joseph's path in these trials saw the Lord's favor on him in the midst of terrible circumstances.
- When Joseph first had a vision, he [perhaps] thought that vision was for his own glory. When that vision finally came true (almost 30 years later) and his brothers were bowing before him, Joseph then said these words: "You intended to harm me, but God intended it for good to accomplish what is now being done, *the saving of many lives*" (Genesis 50:20, italics added).

Joseph's story reveals God's power and character. Do you believe your story reveals these things too?

I do.

Go & See.

Tool 4: Writing a Personal Essay

Personal Essays: Understanding, learning from, and finding value in the moments (both the painful and joyful) in our lives. The aim of this activity is for you to begin to form your memories into stories of hope, provision, heart change, and miracles. Then ultimately, to record them to be passed on from generation to generation so that *all the world may know the hand of the Lord on the earth* (Joshua 4:24).

A personal essay re-creates a specific experience or event in your life using sensory details, specific action, and revealing dialogue to engage readers in a way that makes them feel they are a part of the experience. The objective of the story is to show what you learned from the experience—to recollect, reflect, and display revelations and truths that were birthed from it. A writer does not merely tell a story for personal reasons, but *in order to communicate a larger truth to the reader*; the story is the vehicle on which the truth, often metaphorically, rides.

One more thing to keep in mind as you write is that you will want to ensure you are "breathing life" (2 Timothy 3:16) into your stories by including scripture and biblical truths in them. Incorporating Bible verses into your story can come in the revising process, so don't stress about this part at first. Or you can start your writing process by listing the verses that ring true with the message of your story before you begin so that you can insert them while writing.

First, *Go & See* with fresh eyes what you have recorded on your timeline from Lessons 1 and 2. Pray and ask the Holy Spirit to show you if there is one "stone" that your heart needs you to *Go & See* a deeper understanding of. Or choose a "stone" that highlights a significant moment when God revealed himself to you. A third option is to use the Testimony Writing Prompts (located at the close of this lesson) to help you narrow down your selection.

Next, circle the 1–3 "stones" that most jump out to you. Next to each "stone" you circled, write just one word or phrase that could symbolize the theme or lesson of that experience. If you have not yet labeled the experience with one of the following categories: Creation, Fall, Restoration, or Redemption, then do so before moving on.

Personal Essay Writing Instructions

1. *Go* to the "stones" you circled at the close of the "Digging Deeper" section. Of the three you circled, choose one to write about in story form.

2. *Go* to the "What Is a Personal Essay?" handout and begin working *step by step* through the section titled "Selecting a Topic & Gathering Ideas," using the story and details of the "stone" you chose from step one.

3. After you have gathered ideas, study the rest of the "What Is a Personal Essay?" handout to gain a general understanding of all that is entailed in writing a personal essay.
   In particular, note the last section: **A writer does not merely tell a story for personal reasons, but in order to communicate a larger truth to the reader. The story is the vehicle on which the truth, often metaphorically, rides.**

4. Then create a short personal essay to share at the close of this study. (Keep in mind, most personal essays are less than 750 words.)

5. Once you have your first draft written, *go* back through the "What is a Personal Essay?" handout and see if there are any ways you can revise your writing to meet the style and voice of a personal essay.

6. Then *go* back and find places where you can "breathe life" (2 Timothy 3:16) into your essay by including a Bible passage or biblical truth into the theme of your story. (Some of the verses from this lesson or from another part of this study could be useful to you. *Go & See.*)

7. If you find yourself getting stuck with your writing, ask the Holy Spirit to come join you and give you clarity. If you are still stuck, consider choosing a different "stone" to work with.

A suggested breakdown of these steps is as follows:

- ❏ Day 1: Steps 1 and 2.
- ❏ Day 2: Steps 3 and 4.
- ❏ Day 3: Steps 5 and 6.
- ❏ Days 4–6: Repeat with a new story or revise what you've written.

 ## The Next Step

Each day this week, spend time working on creating a personal essay from an event or experience on your timeline. This may be very challenging, especially to get started, but *see* this time as an invitation from Jesus to **"get away with him by yourself to a quiet place."** And imagine that on the other side of the lake Jesus asks what you have to meet the needs of the people there.

Consider that your story is what you have—your five loaves and two fish. Be expectant that God will take what you have and multiply it. *Believe he will*, and let that bring you freedom to put pen to paper or fingers to keyboard and just start writing.

As you are writing, keep in mind which category the experience you are focusing on is settled under (Creation, Fall, Redemption, or Restoration). Let this help you find scripture and biblical truths to add to the message you are working to convey.

Don't worry about grammar, spelling, punctuation, … none of that! Just worry about getting your ideas down in a somewhat organized manner that communicates how this part of your story reveals a truth about who God is and what he has done, or creates in the mind of the listener a picture that he or she can see is a reminder that the hand of the Lord is mighty and able to save.

Closing

Bravely wrestling with and then recording an impactful life experience can help you share with others a testimony of how God uses one's life experiences to reveal his presence and calling. The Holy Spirit's presence and power are what will lead you to revelation, peace, and instruction. Revealing that power by putting your discoveries on paper helps you share more frequently and naturally the reality of God's active presence on earth, thus helping you fulfill the Great Commission of bringing the gospel to the ends of the earth, potentially beginning with the neighbor next door.

God desires for us to *Go & See* how what we have can meet the needs of the "multitudes" when he miraculously multiplies the little bit we have.
Mark 6:30-44

Themes and life lessons are often found in our mistakes, our disappointments, and our suffering. As you gather up the details of your life, pay close attention to the times when you experienced storms, the wilderness, a desert, or darkness. Seek understanding for how these periods or moments of hardship have built into you a capacity for compassion, passion, repentance, or humility. Then also consider how these experiences have shaped the needs you see in the world and the ways the redemption of these sufferings has given you the power and strength to pursue sharing love, time, talents, or the gospel with others who have been put in your path as a result of your common suffering.

Diamonds are purified by pressure. Heat is required to mold gold into tokens of love and beauty. Clay vases start from dust and water, which is then churned into mud, spun into shape, and baked by fire in order to become a vessel that lasts. Therefore, consider diamonds, gold, and clay as you navigate toward understanding how suffering can lead you to *see* (and articulate) your purpose, talents, and visions. In addition, using metaphors such as these in your writing can help you point to the overcoming power of Christ's work through your story.

Now it is time to *Go & See* what's waiting there for God to reveal to you while you work at setting up a stone of remembrance from the story of your life—a story originally authored by God at the beginning of time. Enjoy the discovery.

Testimony Writing Prompts

If you are like me, it is easier to generate focused ideas when given a specific question to answer. The following list of prompts can help you set aside the "writer's block" (indecision or paralysis in choosing a topic or starting to write) that many writers face when staring at a blank sheet of paper. Let the questions help you begin writing or generate more ideas in the prewriting stages.

1. What experience(s) in your life reveals the faithfulness of God?
2. What experience(s) in your life gives testimony to God's grace?
3. What experience(s) in your life demonstrates God's relentless pursuit of your heart?
4. What experience(s) in your life gives an image of God's abundance?
5. What experience(s) in your life shows God's mercy?
6. What experience(s) in your life points toward the truth of heaven?
7. What experience(s) in your life reveals the magnitude of God and his presence in all the earth?
8. What experience(s) in your life reminds you that God delights in you?
9. What experience(s) in your life made you grow deeper in believing God is in control?
10. What experience(s) in your life shows the importance and necessity of living in relationship with other believers?
11. What experience(s) in your life reveals your failure but God's peace?
12. What experience(s) in your life brings to light the glory in the mundane?
13. What experience(s) in your life turned your heart toward trusting God?
14. What experience(s) in your life brought you unexpected joy?
15. What experience(s) in your life caused you to doubt before you believed?
16. What experience(s) in your life helped you claim a specific promise of God?
17. What experience(s) in your life ruined a lie you had let yourself believe?
18. What experience(s) in your life reminds you to be grateful?
19. What experience(s) in your life changed your plans?
20. What experience(s) in your life broke you but also healed you?

Notes:

What Is a Personal Essay?

	Defining the Personal Essay Genre
Personal Narrative Essay Traits	• Re-creates a specific experience or event in your life (funny, frightening, life-changing encounters, etc.). • Uses sensory details, specific action, and revealing dialogue to bring the experience to life. • Should engage the audience to share in your experiences (cause them to feel what you felt in the moment you are describing). • Shares the details of a specific event or time in your life, emphasizing what you learned from the experience. • Part recollection + part reflection.

	How to Write in the Personal Essay Genre
Selecting a Topic & Gathering Ideas	• Brainstorm using a prewriting activity that helps you recall incidents in your life you think are worth sharing/fit the definition of a personal essay. (Your timeline from Lessons 1 & 2, and your reflection from Lesson 3.) • List the top 2–3 experiences that best fit the description of your current assignment. (Steps in Lesson 4.) • Then, next to each experience, jot down important details, words, or actions that describe the experience/memory. (Steps in Lesson 4.) • Types of details: 　○ Sensory: What you saw, heard, smelled, tasted, or touched. 　○ Actions: What you did or experienced. 　○ Dialogue: What people said to each other. 　○ Reflective: What you thought or felt about the experience. • It may be helpful to write about each experience by finishing these sentences: 　○ (The experience/memory) makes me feel … 　○ (The experience/memory) causes me to … 　○ (The experience/memory) concerns me because … 　○ (The experience/memory) has taught me … • Don't forget to decide on the tone you will use: How do you want your audience to feel at the end of the essay (sad, humored, reflective, grateful, amused, etc.)?

Organizing	• Since narratives are usually told in chronological order, you can use a timeline to organize your details. • Your opening should grab the audience's attention, the middle should re-create the experience, and the ending should reflect on the experience.
Writing	• Hooking the audience: Start your narrative right in the action. Doing so will immediately help get your audience's attention. (Leave backstory out, or place limited details later in the story.) • Keeping the audience interested: Let the audience feel as if the experience is unfolding right in front of them. (This is where showing via sensory, action, and dialogue details comes in.) • After getting the first draft down, revise your work using the following questions as your guide: 　○ Does my writing/words reveal the importance of the experience? 　○ Have I organized the details/words effectively? 　○ Does my tone fit my topic? 　○ Did I choose the best possible words to convey my message and engage my audience? • Make revisions where necessary.

	Desired Characteristics of a Personal Essay
Why and when to use a personal essay?	• The personal essay genre is profoundly respected among writers because it is *authentic, vulnerable,* and *poignant.* • Allow your reader into your life. • Themes of *romance, family, growing up, nature, spirituality, neighbors, home, war,* and *death* are common experiences that, when shared, can create a sense of connection, community, and understanding between the writer and his or her audience.
Relating to Your Audience (Communal Relevance)	A writer does not merely tell a story for personal reasons, but *in order to communicate a larger truth to the reader.* The story is the vehicle on which the truth, often metaphorically, rides. The personal essay argues, in a way, that the beauty associated with being human can often best be expressed through the sharing of stories. Thus, writers should seek to reveal true experiences, moments of relevance, and believed lessons learned with an authentic, believable voice. **At the end of the essay, the reader has the right to ask, "So why is this important or relevant to me?" and have it answered.**

(adapted from *Writer's Inc. Write for College Handbook*)

Lesson:5

Understanding Your Unique Design

Purpose and Context

God desires for us to Go & See how what we have can meet the needs of the "multitudes" when he miraculously multiplies the little bit we have.

Mark 6:30-44

We have all been given talents that we are asked to invest [multiply] until the day our master returns and asks us to give an account for what we did with what he gave us.

Matthew 25:14-30

We are forgetful. Thus, we need to set-up "stones of remembrance" as markers of God's faithfulness, strength and involvement in our journey.

Joshua 4

Introduction

We have all been given gifts (skills, talents, experiences, relationships, grace) to be used to do the work of heaven on earth. God has "talents" for each of us, and we are commanded to multiply them until his return (Matthew 25:14–30). This is easier said than done, for sure. Yet knowing your unique design is paramount to running the race marked out for you. You have been given an exclusive combination of natural talents, spiritual gifts, and personality traits that are assigned only to you. This session is designed to help you see more clearly how who you are, the way you've been designed, is specific to how you will be used for the glory of God and to impact both earth and heaven.

Understanding your unique design can be challenging and time-consuming. In fact, it may require some endurance and awkward moments of seeking the input of others. Be confident, however, that it is worth it because your creator-Father desires for you to take joy in being the rare gem that you are. He desires for you to experience the fullness of peace and freedom that comes through the confidence gained in living out of who you were designed to be from the start. When you live from this place of understanding and wholeness, you will discover that—like the loaves of bread and fish multiplying to feed the five thousand—God will start multiplying what you have to meet the needs of the "multitudes" you are asked to provide nourishment to.

I pray that this lesson will help you *see* that working at excavating and understanding your natural talents, spiritual gifts, and personality traits (along with your testimony—*your life's timeline and story*) can propel you forward from where you are right now.

Why aim to move forward?

Because as Christ-followers, we are called to a dynamic, not a stagnant life. Yes, sometimes fear, doubt, or simply a lack of understanding of our unique design's purpose can hold us back from moving forward. But you have the power to overcome all of these. So before

We have all been given talents that we are asked to invest [multiply] until the day our master returns and asks us to give an account for what we did with what he gave us.
Matthew 25:14-30

starting this session, pray and ask the Holy Spirit to come and remove any burdens or barriers that might try to hold you back from excavating the beautiful talents, gifts, and traits that God asks you to *Go & See* as the "*bread and fish*" he wants to *multiply through you* to meet your needs and the needs of those around you.

 ## Reflection & Application

If you need to refresh your memory on the scriptural rooting for this study, take a couple of minutes to *Go & See* what is recorded in Mark 6:30–44 and Matthew 25:14–30. Keep these passages in mind as you navigate this lesson because the metaphors, contexts, and characters in the stories help us see the necessity of taking seriously the act of *Going & Seeing* what we have, as little as it may seem. It isn't until we *see* clearly what we have that we can then begin investing what we have been given. First, we *go*. Next, we *see*. Then we spend time working with the "talents" we discover in ways that enable us to invest in meeting the needs of others, as an act of worship to God. Investing is our end goal.

Why is this our end goal?

Because scripture tells us that as Christians our primary, all-inclusive purpose is to obey the teachings Jesus gave to his disciples. All that was recorded as instructions to the disciples in the New Testament was set there for us to have in order to do likewise. We are his disciples. As such, our lives are to give witness to God's presence, power, and love at work in all the earth (Acts 1:8). Therefore, we have each been given "talents" purposed to increase the work of God's restoration plan.

Your participation in this divine restoration plan is not optional. This restoration plan is meant to center your life. And when your motives, actions, and vision are aligned with his plan for restoration, then you will flourish because participating in this plan is your ultimate purpose on this earth.

Before we dig in deeper, it is important to start by looking at what the Bible instructs us to do as it pertains to spiritual gifts. Take a few minutes and *Go & See* what is written in 1 Corinthians 12:1–31. Highlight anything that sticks out to you.

Did you *see* the following?

- There are different kinds of gifts—ways of serving and jobs to be fulfilled—but the same Spirit of God gives the gifts and accomplishes the work.
- Gifts are for the *common* (unified) good--to unify the work of the Body of Christ.
- The variety of *gifts* is intentional and purposed.
- Here is the list for quick reference:

- the ability to deliver messages of wisdom,
- the ability to deliver messages of knowledge,
- faith,
- gifts of healing,
- miraculous powers,
- prophecy,
- distinguishing between spirits, and
- speaking in tongues.

- The body has many parts, arranged by God to function as *one unit.*
- The *appointments*—leadership areas--are also intentionally varied by design and are given (*as gifts*) from above.
- Here is the list for quick reference:
  - apostles,
  - prophets,
  - teachers,
  - workers of miracles,
  - those gifted in healing,
  - those who help others,
  - administrators, and
  - those who speak in different tongues.

Every good and perfect gift is from above, coming down from the Father of the heavenly lights, who does not change like shifting shadows.

James 1:17

Now, *go* read 1 Corinthians 13. Then, using the questions below, take several minutes to reflect on scripture to *see* its application to your life. Pull out your journal and get to a quiet place of mind. Then answer each question as fully as possible. Check off each one as you go.

☐ **1)** Why does the love chapter immediately follow the "gift assignment" chapter?

☐ **2)** What evidence from this passage (or other parts of the Bible) help you *see* that to know and use your gifts *is not* optional but rather an instruction to obey?

☐ **3)** Make a list of the gifts (*natural talents, spiritual gifts, personality traits,* and *life experiences*) you have seen God use to reveal to you his presence, power, and love at work in your life or the lives of people around you.

    ☐ **a)** Describe a time when God used your gifts to restore or refresh others.

    ☐ **b)** Describe a time when God used the gifts he's given *you* to restore *you.*

    ☐ **c)** Describe a time when God used your gifts to build up another person's gifts.

Notes:

Notes:

Digging Deeper

We are called. We have gifts. You are called. You have talents to invest. We have specific and glorious appointments for such a time as this. What if you looked at the journey of discovering your calling as if it were Christmas morning? You run down the stairs and dig under the tree. Then you find all the gifts with your name on them. Next, you start unwrapping them to **see what you have been given**.

There are a couple of differences between the typical gift we are given under the Christmas tree and the gifts we are given to fulfill our calling. First, the gifts we are given to fulfill our calling are not intended just for personal use. They are given to us for the "common good," so that we can help one another *reveal God* to the people we know *in our portion of the world*.

Second, the typical gift you receive on your birthday or Christmas morning does not multiply itself—unless of course you are the type of person who receives seeds or trees as gifts. Unlike material or man-made gifts, the gifts given to us from God are multiplied and increased by the work of the Holy Spirit living in us. This multiplication is only accomplished through Christ, who gives us grace, strength, and power to **invest all that we are and have into doing all that we are designed to be and do.**

In 2 Thessalonians, Paul points out very clearly the main reason you are charged to *Go & See* what you have been given and then use the gifts and "talents" in your life to live out your purpose and vision, so that the name of our Lord Jesus will be *glorified in you* and *you in him*.

> We constantly pray for you, that our God may count you worthy of his calling, and that by his power he may fulfill every good purpose of yours and every act prompted by your faith. We pray *this so* that the name of our Lord Jesus may be *glorified in you*, and *you in Him*, according to the grace of our God and the Lord Jesus Christ. (2 Thessalonians 1:11–12 NIV 1984, italics added)

This call to lift the name of Jesus high in our lives, so that the world can see his light through us—that our lives may be illuminated by his glory—is a corporate calling with individual assignments. All our *resources, natural talents, spiritual gifts,* and *personality traits* are to *build up, support,* and *advance* the assignments of the corporate body of believers. But the ways in which the gifts work within the lives of each believer will be as unique as the snowflakes that fall from the sky: no two alike in shape and size, yet alike in color, texture, and beauty. And when thousands of them cover a landscape, it glimmers and shines in the sun (pun 100 percent intended!), revealing awe and wonder that attract the observer to our creator-God.

Rebekah Lyons, in her *Be Still and Know Study,* puts it this way: within this corporate calling, we all have unique expressions. Throughout history—and still today—God places specific assignments in our lives. He created each of us with talents and burdens to advance his kingdom work on earth. This alone is all we need to believe in order to live our purpose right now.

In addition, corporate and individual callings are part of our destiny. Each generation, people group, and person has been uniquely created and strategically located to fulfill a purpose in the time and the place they were set in. Christine Cain, at IF:Gathering 2018, put it this way: "If you are breathing on this earth, you are called to something right now because he put you here right now." This is as true now as it was in the past. Choose to believe it every day.

And on the days when you have doubts, consider these "heroes" of the Bible and how they were used by God in their time and place to accomplish deliverance and freedom for others: Moses, Joseph, David, Daniel, Esther, Deborah, Rahab, Mary, and Jesus. (Who else can you think of?) All of these people show us what it looks like to be set in a time and a place to lead a people, save lives, advance the kingdom, and storm the gates of hell. The same is true for you and for me! We are given the stories of these imperfect but chosen men and women so that we can have the courage and strength to follow their lead. There is no time like the present to start living like Esthers in our generation!

Paul reminds us of our purposed destiny in 2 Timothy 1:9. Here his words stress the truth that our design and purpose were set in us at creation: "not according to our works, but according to His own purpose and grace which was given to us in Christ Jesus before time began" (NKJV). Yes, before time began, God had you designed to be who you are, set in your places and realm of influence, and doing what you are doing. *All these details of your life are gifts.* These giftings come from a good and amazing Giver. They don't stand alone under a tree. They are not mysterious packages from an unknown sender. But they do **need to be found**, unwrapped, examined, offered up to Jesus, and set under the power of the Spirit in order to be used well.

So before you begin exploring the gifts and examining the ways in which they can be used (or if you are simply struggling to *see* the gifts given to you), *stop and seek the Giver.* Believe and state as truth that you are gifted for a purpose and there is a vision written on your soul. Deliberately *stop* and remind your soul that your life was set into motion before time, and nothing can separate you from the design imprinted on you. Ask your heavenly Father to be present as you *Go & See* what he has already given you to advance the restoration plan of his kingdom.

Now, with all of the above in mind, seek to *see* the unwrapping of your gifts as an act of love toward the Giver of the gifts. Look at these as gifts to be *valued*, *enjoyed*, and *used* as described in 1 Thessalonians 5:16–21:

But they do need to be found, unwrapped, examined, offered up to Jesus, and set under the power of the Spirit in order to be used well.

Rejoice always and delight in your faith; be unceasing and persistent in prayer; in every situation [no matter what the circumstances] be thankful and continually give thanks to God; for this is the will of God for you in Christ Jesus. Do not quench [subdue, or be unresponsive to the working and guidance of] the [Holy] Spirit. Do not scorn or reject gifts of prophecy or prophecies [spoken revelations—words of instruction or exhortation or warning]. But test all things carefully [so you can recognize what is good]. *Hold firmly to that which is good.* (AMP, italics added)

 ## Tool 5: Excavating & Taking Inventory of Your Gifts

Excavating & Taking Inventory of Your Gifts: Tools to help you see the "talents" set in you by God and nurtured by others and your experiences.

As you step into this process of excavating and taking inventory of your gifts, approach each as you would a beautifully wrapped gift handed to you to be opened. Let the Lord's joy be your strength as you pursue understanding who you are, whose you are, and how you are uniquely designed for fulfilling your rare and needed purpose for this time and place—which just might be the saving of lives.

There are many ways to unwrap a gift. And depending on the size or shape of the gift, one may use a different strategy to unpack it. So, we are going to use a variety of tools to *Go & See* what the Giver of the gifts has given to each of us.

It is important with each gift that is unwrapped that you pause and *Go & See* in the deepest parts of your heart *the reasons* you have been given the gifts that are displayed before you. By this I mean, asking for revelation to gain an understanding of *how your natural talents, spiritual gifts, and personality traits point you to your purpose and vision.*

Also, remember when you go hunting to find those reasons, you can know you are on the right track if those reasons you find are rooted in and supported by the words of scripture. If you are unsure, seek counsel from a parent, pastor, or older adult you trust who knows the Bible well.

In this process, doubt and disbelief may knock at the door of your confidence. Be on guard. Do not let doubt creep in and rob you of your motivation. It is worth your time to enter this journey of seeking and understanding. *Going* and *seeing* is a necessary part of your faith journey. Claim and believe this. Enter with caution and in relationship with others who know you well.

Why?

Because discernment is also necessary for understanding your gifts and divine purpose. Discernment is the ability to *see* and decide between truth and error, right and wrong. It is also the process of checking our thinking and ideas against what is biblically true. In order to know what is biblically true, we need to be reading the Bible and bringing our questions about purpose and giftings to God, asking him to reveal and instruct. We also need to have candid conversations with others who know the Bible and can help us to "examine everything carefully; hold fast to that which is good" (1 Thessalonians 5:21 NASB).

To reiterate, discernment is found in close proximity to God, studying his words, and by inviting in the revealing power of the Holy Spirit. Only in close relationship with Christ do we see the truest versions of ourselves. *He delights in revealing to us our unique talents and assignments—talents and assignments that equip us to go into all the world sharing the good news of Christ, who saves, restores, redeems, and brings hope and peace.* Sometimes he uses the Bible, other times he may use prayer, in other seasons he may use circumstances, and most often he uses other believers to help us **see who we are and what we are uniquely gifted to invest** in during our one life here on this earth.

 ## Instructions

First, invite the Holy Spirit into the following reflection and analysis activities. Work through as many as you have time for over the coming week. (There is one activity for each day of the week.) Try super-duper hard to carve out time daily for these activities because they will help you greatly in understanding your unique design and affirm you in who you are in Christ.

- ❑ **Day 1**: Review your **Personal Timeline** from Lesson 1, and work through the **Experiences Reflection Activity**. Focus on the truth that God's hand in our stories points us to passions, burdens, and purpose.
- ❑ **Day 2**: Work through the **Excavating Calling Activity**. Take action and dig into areas of your life that help you *see* how who you are brings clarity to your purpose within the body of Christ and your specific assignments (vision) based on your unique design.
- ❑ **Day 3**: Complete the **What Others See in You Questionnaire**. This will require you to get coffee with or phone a friend (or two) and ask them to help you see yourself more clearly by answering a few questions. Brave through the awkwardness of extending this invite because it will be worth it.
- ❑ **Day 4:** Complete the **Spiritual Gifts Survey**. Or use the online tool at **SpiritualGiftsTest.com**.
  - ❑ Reflect and process your discoveries using the Spiritual Gifts Inventory & Reflection Guide

❏ **Day 5:** Complete the ***Processing Your Personality Type Grid***. This task requires you to look at the following couple online tools to help you make discoveries.

  ❏ The 16personalities.com site takes you through the Myers-Briggs personality type Personality Test.

  ❏ The https://www.jesusfilm.org/about/learn-more/mbti-download.html site takes you through the Discipleship Guide for the 16 Myers-Briggs Personality Types. *This guide is my absolute favorite tool* for producing understanding, courage, and *aha* moments.

 # The Next Step

Now that you have a wealth of words to define and describe your unique design, it is time to enter that data into long-term memory and give the Holy Spirit permission to help you **seek vision for investing** in the gifts and "talents" you have been given. I have discovered that the best way to do this on my own is to pray, reflect, and write. Do these first.

Pray, reflect, and write down your discoveries. Using the Your Unique Design Artifact (at the end of this lesson), take 30–45 minutes to write out what you *see* as the exclusive combination of natural talents, spiritual gifts, and personality traits assigned only to you to enjoy and invest. This could be in paragraph or bullet form. Or you could get creative and use a graphic organizer or pictures. The goal is for you to create an artifact that helps you to see your "two fish and five loaves" (Mark 6:30–44) and the "talents" (Matthew 25:14–30) given to you by your master to invest continually until his return.

The second step toward giving the Holy Spirit permission to help you invest your "talents" is to invite in the voices of other members of the body of Christ to pray over you, process with you, and dig deeper into the discoveries you have made. Call or message a pastor or other church leader, counselor, or friend, and set up a meeting time to invite them into helping you understand how to invest your gifts within your church, home, workplace, and community. Bring to the meeting the work you have done in excavating and taking inventory of your gifts. Share what you've found, and simply ask, "Can you help me live into my unique design?"

Then move in the direction God prompts you to *go*.

Closing

There are a variety of ways God chooses to reveal himself to us. There are a variety of ways for us to *Go & See* what gifts he has given to us to increase our joy, strength, and effectiveness in meeting the needs of those around us. But most essential to our ability to use our gifts to live lives of purpose rooted in who he has made us to be is first to believe, really believe, that a good, good Father made me and made you in unique and beautiful ways *for this time and in this place* to *increase his glory* on the earth and *to demonstrate his great love for and delight in us.* And then to begin doing the work of *Going & See*ing all the "talents" and gifts he has given you and asks you to invest until his return.

Persist in unwrapping these gifts. Yes, persistence and perseverance will likely be required. Not because God is a tricky jokester who wraps a gift seventeen times just to make it hard to find the gem inside. But because we are in a fallen world, and the devil would love nothing more than to stress you out or confuse you as you seek to understand more clearly who you are, whose you are, and how you are designed beautifully and uniquely to bring Jesus to people.

So, as you *Go & See* what gifts he is asking you to unwrap, trust that even if you can't *see* them right away, they are there. Seek him. Ask him to reveal his gifts and purposes for you to you. *He already knows them and has a plan for the ways you will use them.* There is freedom in being in his holy presence and trusting that he reveals. Rest there, knowing that you have a tailor-made package of gifts set aside just for you to be able to put love into action—to bring glory to the King of heaven and earth. Claim, believe, and make this your mantra: "Every good and perfect gift is from above, coming down from the Father of the heavenly lights" (James 1:17).

He is talking about you.

He is speaking of your design.

Go & See.

Experiences Reflection* Grid

Using your timeline from Lessons 1 and 2, identify a highlight from each life stage. Highlights are times when you felt joy or comfort in what you were doing, who you were with or pivotal moments that shaped your view of yourself, God, or the world.

Before beginning, ask the Holy Spirit to bring to your memory answers to this question: In what moments of my life do I remember being proud and satisfied?

Do not overthink it. Just write down the first things that come to mind.

Once you've filled in the "Highlight" column, go back and fill in the next column with a couple of descriptive words to answer the question: what specifically about these moments was satisfying to you?

Here are some more questions to get you thinking:

- What were you great at?
- What did you love to do?
- What made you stand in awe?
- Whom did you love, and why did you love them?
- What experiences helped you learn something about yourself?
- What did you dream about?

Life Stage (approximate)	Highlight	Satisfaction
Example	*Being outside doing chores with my dad.*	*Accomplishing a necessary task. Being of help.*
Ages 0–7		
Ages 8–12		
Ages 13–18		
Ages 19–24		
Ages 25–34		
Ages 35–44		
Ages 45–54		
Ages 55–64		
Ages 65+		

*Adapted from Jennie Allen's, *Restless Study*

Excavating Calling Grid

In her book, *More than Enchanting*, Jo Saxton recommends taking a closer look at where you are right now to begin excavating a picture of your gifts and calling. Use the questions below to *Go & See* what God wants to show you in these areas of your life.

Area to Reflect Upon	My Personal Reflection & Thoughts
Spending time with God: • In what ways have I been seeking and listening by spending time with God? • Is what I am dreaming about something that reflects God's values and priorities in some way? How? Why?	
What's in your heart? What's on your mind? • In what ways do my passions, emotions, intellect, will, and personality point to my purpose? • What thoughts and ideas buzz around in my mind when I am day-dreaming?	

Ask the right questions: • What do I want to be said of me when my life is over? • What does it mean to begin living my life with the end of my life in mind?	
Friends: • What do my friends and family members say I am good at?	
Attending to the life we have: Just because it may be obvious doesn't mean it's not from God. • What about the life I already have is exciting, brings joy, and helps me feel close to God? • How can I imagine my dream job also being God's purpose for my life?	
(Super) Natural Talent: • What do I enjoy? • What am I good at? • What seems to come naturally for me?	

Built based on the writing of Jo Saxton in chapter 3 of *More than Enchanting*

What Others See in You Questionnaire

How we *see* ourselves is often not a completely accurate picture of who we are and the impact we have on the world around us. So put your bravery on, and invite one or two people in to offer you the gift of perspective. You can do this over the phone, over coffee, on a walk, or in writing. Know that this just might be the most encouraging experience you will have throughout this study. So don't skip this activity. Here are some good questions to choose from. Ask as few or as many as you like.

Question	Answer
When have you seen me operating in my sweet spot?	
What do you think I do well?	

In what ways have you seen me grow and develop my gifts in the last few years?	
Have I helped you grow? If so, how?	
Of the gifts in the chart below, which do you think would be my top 3–5? Can you remember a time you saw me operating in one or more of these gifts?	

Prophecy (1 Cor. 12:10; Rom. 12:6)	Teaching (1 Cor. 12:28; Rom. 12:7; Eph. 4:11)
Exhortation (Rom. 12:8)	Instruction (wisdom & knowledge) (1 Cor. 12:8, 28)
Service (1 Cor. 12:28; Rom. 12:7)	Giving (Rom. 12:8)
Leadership (Rom. 12:8)	Mercy (Rom. 12:8)
Apostleship (1 Cor. 12:28; Eph. 4:11)	Faith (1 Cor. 12:9)
Working Miracles (1 Cor. 12:28)	Discernment (1 Cor. 12:10)
Administration (1 Cor. 12:28)	Hospitality (1 Pet. 4:9)
Evangelism (Eph. 4:11)	Shepherding (pastoring) (Eph. 4:11)

Adapted from Jennie Allen's *Restless Study*

Post-Conversation Reflection

Take some time to read over the answers you have written down from the **What Others See in You Questionnaire**. Pray, asking the Holy Spirit to help you discern and understand your perspective of yourself, others' perspective of you, and most importantly His point of view as your designer.

Then record answers to the following questions.

1. How did what you hear align with your perspective of yourself?
2. How did what you hear differ from your perspective of yourself?
3. What do you think God is trying to get you to *see* through the differences and similarities of the perspectives of others in comparison to your perspective of yourself?
4. Describe a natural talent, spiritual gift, or life experience the conversation(s) helped you *see* as a signpost to guide you to your unique purpose and vision.
5. Did you have any "aha" moments? If so, record those below.

Spiritual Gifts Survey

Below is a survey to help you discover some of your spiritual gifts. This is not a test, so there are no wrong answers. This is just a tool to get you started. To reiterate, this is one tool that can help you in your discovery processes, but the scripture and the Holy Spirit, along with prayer and conversations with friends who know you and Jesus well, are also of utmost importance. Work through each step below to begin your discovery.

Step 1: Carefully, read through the questions below.

Questions regarding your initial response: (1) Which of these gifts excites you? (2) Which ones catch your attention and make you want to know everything about them and make them your own? (3) How have you responded when you've seen other people practice using these gifts?

Questions related to your experiences: (1) What experiences have you had with some of these gifts? (2) When faced with practicing one, did you rise to the occasion with joy or hunker down and get through it? As Christians, we participate in all these duties at different times, but when God gives us the spiritual gift for it, we often feel supernatural fulfillment.

Questions regarding using spiritual gifts: (1) How have others seen and/or encouraged you in your gifts in the past? (2) What was the outcome when you practiced using that gift? This third set of questions is key. Since we practice our spiritual gifts for the body, other members of the body become our best reflection for understanding our gifts. They see God's supernatural work through us.

In a nutshell: (1) What do you know to be true about yourself in this area? (2) What has been your experience when you've served in this way? (3) What have others affirmed in you?

Step 2: Read through each spiritual gift description in the survey.

Step 3: After you have read through each spiritual gift description, then go back and place a checkmark next to any boxes that describe your response to the description.

Step 4: Review your responses, and note which gifts you have checked the most boxes for.

Step 5: Pray and ask God to show you how to gain more understanding of your gifts and how to invest in using them in daily and sacrificial ways.

Step 6: Complete the Spiritual Gifts Inventory & Reflection Guide.

The Gift of Prophecy: proclaiming God's truth to build up the body. This doesn't necessarily mean prediction (in fact, it rarely does) but recognizing particular, God-given truth in a specific situation, as it is consistent with the Christian faith, and revealing it to his people to encourage them (1 Cor. 12:10; Rom. 12:6). (Check all boxes that apply to you.)

- ❑ The description of this gift excites me.
- ❑ This gift catches my attention, making me want to know everything about it and how to use it to build others up.
- ❑ When I see others using this gift, I wonder how I could do that too.
- ❑ I have some positive experiences with using this gift.
- ❑ When I have used this gift, it has brought me joy.
- ❑ Others have encouraged me to use this gift on one or more occasions.
- ❑ I have seen positive outcomes in others' lives as a result of using this gift.

The Gift of Service *(helps)*: recognizing and caring for physical or material needs. Do not mind working behind the scenes (1 Cor. 12:28; Rom. 12:7). (Check all boxes that apply to you.)

- ❑ The description of this gift excites me.
- ❑ This gift catches my attention, making me want to know everything about it and how to use it to build others up.
- ❑ When I see others using this gift, I wonder how I could do that too.
- ❑ I have some positive experiences with using this gift.
- ❑ When I have used this gift, it has brought me joy.
- ❑ Others have encouraged me to use this gift on one or more occasions.
- ❑ I have seen positive outcomes in others' lives as a result of using this gift.

The Gift of Teaching: communicating the truth of scripture in a way that others find clarifying, applicable, and inspiring (1 Cor. 12:28; Rom. 12:7; Eph. 4:11). (Check all boxes that apply to you.)

- ❑ The description of this gift excites me.
- ❑ This gift catches my attention, making me want to know everything about it and how to use it to build others up.
- ❑ When I see others using this gift, I wonder how I could do that too.
- ❑ I have some positive experiences with using this gift.
- ❑ When I have used this gift, it has brought me joy.
- ❑ Others have encouraged me to use this gift on one or more occasions.
- ❑ I have seen positive outcomes in others' lives as a result of using this gift.

The Gift of Exhortation: encouraging, consoling, and counseling others to live out their faith through suffering and hardship (Rom. 12:8). (Check all boxes that apply to you.)

- ❑ The description of this gift excites me.
- ❑ This gift catches my attention, making me want to know everything about it and how to use it to build others up.
- ❑ When I see others using this gift, I wonder how I could do that too.
- ❑ I have some positive experiences with using this gift.
- ❑ When I have used this gift, it has brought me joy.
- ❑ Others have encouraged me to use this gift on one or more occasions.
- ❑ I have seen positive outcomes in others' lives as a result of using this gift.

The Gift of Giving: contributing personal resources to help others with generosity. "With generosity" here doesn't mean "in large amounts," but gets to the heart of how we share: with a single-minded purpose, which is God's glory, not for recognition, not with condescension, and not to gain an upper hand relationally or politically. Because this doesn't speak to amounts, a person could be poor and generous. Early Christians often were (Rom. 12:8). (Check all boxes that apply to you.)

- ❑ The description of this gift excites me.
- ❑ This gift catches my attention, making me want to know everything about it and how to use it to build others up.
- ❑ When I see others using this gift, I wonder how I could do that too.
- ❑ I have some positive experiences with using this gift.
- ❑ When I have used this gift, it has brought me joy.
- ❑ Others have encouraged me to use this gift on one or more occasions.
- ❑ I have seen positive outcomes in others' lives as a result of using this gift.

The Gift of Leadership: overseeing a group, often by discerning God's purpose, communicating that purpose, and motivating others to serve for that God-given purpose (Rom. 12:8). (Check all boxes that apply to you.)

- ❑ The description of this gift excites me.
- ❑ This gift catches my attention, making me want to know everything about it and how to use it to build others up.
- ❑ When I see others using this gift, I wonder how I could do that too.
- ❑ I have some positive experiences with using this gift.
- ❑ When I have used this gift, it has brought me joy.
- ❑ Others have encouraged me to use this gift on one or more occasions.
- ❑ I have seen positive outcomes in others' lives as a result of using this gift.

The Gift of Showing Mercy: acts of compassionate concern for those often overlooked, such as the sick, elderly, disabled, and poor (Rom. 12:8). (Check all boxes that apply to you.)

- ❑ The description of this gift excites me.
- ❑ This gift catches my attention, making me want to know everything about it and how to use it to build others up.
- ❑ When I see others using this gift, I wonder how I could do that too.
- ❑ I have some positive experiences with using this gift.
- ❑ When I have used this gift, it has brought me joy.
- ❑ Others have encouraged me to use this gift on one or more occasions.
- ❑ I have seen positive outcomes in others' lives as a result of using this gift.

The Gift of Instruction *(wisdom and knowledge)*: we can't be sure what Paul meant by the "utterance of wisdom" and the "utterance of knowledge," but they both have to do with instructing believers. "Utterance of wisdom" may mean understanding the reality of things with maturity and how to practically apply scripture in everyday life, and "utterance of knowledge" may have to do with discovering and communicating God's mysteries, perhaps with supernatural perception (1 Cor. 12:8 ESV). (Check all boxes that apply to you.)

- ❑ The description of this gift excites me.
- ❑ This gift catches my attention, making me want to know everything about it and how to use it to build others up.
- ❑ When I see others using this gift, I wonder how I could do that too.
- ❑ I have some positive experiences with using this gift.
- ❑ When I have used this gift, it has brought me joy.
- ❑ Others have encouraged me to use this gift on one or more occasions.
- ❑ I have seen positive outcomes in others' lives as a result of using this gift.

The Gift of Faith: all believers have some measure of trust in God, but God has given an extra dose of faith to others. Those with this gift have an extraordinary confidence in God's vision for their reality (1 Cor. 12:9). (Check all boxes that apply to you.)

- ❏ The description of this gift excites me.
- ❏ This gift catches my attention, making me want to know everything about it and how to use it to build others up.
- ❏ When I see others using this gift, I wonder how I could do that too.
- ❏ I have some positive experiences with using this gift.
- ❏ When I have used this gift, it has brought me joy.
- ❏ Others have encouraged me to use this gift on one or more occasions.
- ❏ I have seen positive outcomes in others' lives as a result of using this gift.

The Gift of Healing: supernaturally healing those who are hurt physically, psychologically, or emotionally and restoring them to health. This is separate from the good but natural talents of doctors, nurses, and counselors as this has a supernatural element (1 Cor. 12:9, 28). (Check all boxes that apply to you.)

- ❏ The description of this gift excites me.
- ❏ This gift catches my attention, making me want to know everything about it and how to use it to build others up.
- ❏ When I see others using this gift, I wonder how I could do that too.
- ❏ I have some positive experiences with using this gift.
- ❏ When I have used this gift, it has brought me joy.
- ❏ Others have encouraged me to use this gift on one or more occasions.
- ❏ I have seen positive outcomes in others' lives as a result of using this gift.

The Gift of Working Miracles: the ability to accomplish mighty acts outside the course of natural events to testify to God's presence and power (1 Cor. 12:10, 28). (Check all boxes that apply to you.)

- ❏ The description of this gift excites me.
- ❏ This gift catches my attention, making me want to know everything about it and how to use it to build others up.
- ❏ When I see others using this gift, I wonder how I could do that too.
- ❏ I have some positive experiences with using this gift.
- ❏ When I have used this gift, it has brought me joy.
- ❏ Others have encouraged me to use this gift on one or more occasions.
- ❏ I have seen positive outcomes in others' lives as a result of using this gift.

The Gift of Discernment: the ability to discern between counterfeit spirits and the Holy Spirit, between false teaching and true, especially in the presence of a prophecy. Thus, God sends some to speak out his truth and some to confirm whether a prophecy came from God or from a deceptive spirit (1 Cor. 12:10, 28). (Check all boxes that apply to you.)

- ❏ The description of this gift excites me.
- ❏ This gift catches my attention, making me want to know everything about it and how to use it to build others up.
- ❏ When I see others using this gift, I wonder how I could do that too.
- ❏ I have some positive experiences with using this gift.
- ❏ When I have used this gift, it has brought me joy.
- ❏ Others have encouraged me to use this gift on one or more occasions.
- ❏ I have seen positive outcomes in others' lives as a result of using this gift.

The Gift of Tongues: the ability to speak in or interpret a language not naturally learned. Paul clarifies that for this to be uplifting for the church (1 Cor. 14:6–12), the gift of tongues must be accompanied by an interpretation. (Check all boxes that apply to you.)

- ❏ The description of this gift excites me.
- ❏ This gift catches my attention, making me want to know everything about it and how to use it to build others up.
- ❏ When I see others using this gift, I wonder how I could do that too.
- ❏ I have some positive experiences with using this gift.
- ❏ When I have used this gift, it has brought me joy.
- ❏ Others have encouraged me to use this gift on one or more occasions.
- ❏ I have seen positive outcomes in others' lives as a result of using this gift.

The Gift of Administration: steering a ministry by organizing resources and people and implementing plans (1 Cor. 12:28). (Check all boxes that apply to you.)

- ❏ The description of this gift excites me.
- ❏ This gift catches my attention, making me want to know everything about it and how to use it to build others up.
- ❏ When I see others using this gift, I wonder how I could do that too.
- ❏ I have some positive experiences with using this gift.
- ❏ When I have used this gift, it has brought me joy.
- ❏ Others have encouraged me to use this gift on one or more occasions.
- ❏ I have seen positive outcomes in others' lives as a result of using this gift.

The Gift of Evangelism: effectively sharing the gospel to lead people to Christ (Eph. 4:11). (Check all boxes that apply to you.)

- ❏ The description of this gift excites me.
- ❏ This gift catches my attention, making me want to know everything about it and how to use it to build others up.
- ❏ When I see others using this gift, I wonder how I could do that too.
- ❏ I have some positive experiences with using this gift.
- ❏ When I have used this gift, it has brought me joy.
- ❏ Others have encouraged me to use this gift on one or more occasions.
- ❏ I have seen positive outcomes in others' lives as a result of using this gift.

The Gift of Shepherding (pastoring): spiritually leading God's people by guiding, nourishing, protecting, and caring for them (Eph. 4:11). (Check all boxes that apply to you.)

- ❏ The description of this gift excites me.
- ❏ This gift catches my attention, making me want to know everything about it and how to use it to build others up.
- ❏ When I see others using this gift, I wonder how I could do that too.
- ❏ I have some positive experiences with using this gift.
- ❏ When I have used this gift, it has brought me joy.
- ❏ Others have encouraged me to use this gift on one or more occasions.
- ❏ I have seen positive outcomes in others' lives as a result of using this gift.

The Gift of Hospitality: the ability to make visitors, guests, and strangers feel at ease, often using one's home to entertain guests. Persons with this gift welcome and invite in new members into the church body (1 Pet. 4:9). (Check all boxes that apply to you.)

- ❏ The description of this gift excites me.
- ❏ This gift catches my attention, making me want to know everything about it and how to use it to build others up.
- ❏ When I see others using this gift, I wonder how I could do that too.
- ❏ I have some positive experiences with using this gift.
- ❏ When I have used this gift, it has brought me joy.
- ❏ Others have encouraged me to use this gift on one or more occasions.
- ❏ I have seen positive outcomes in others' lives as a result of using this gift.

Now that you have completed the survey, thoughtfully answer the questions below:

1. The spiritual gifts I am beginning to *see* in my life are:

   ☐ _____

   ☐ _____

   ☐ _____

2. After prayer and worship, I am beginning to sense that God is asking me to use the following spiritual gifts:

   ☐ _____

   ☐ _____

   ☐ _____

3. I am not sure how God wants me to use the following gifts:

   ☐ _____

   ☐ _____

   ☐ _____

4. Am I committed to prayer, worship, and seeking wisdom and opportunities to invest in using the gifts of the spirit given to me from God?

   ☐ Yes

   ☐ Unsure

   ☐ Why? _____

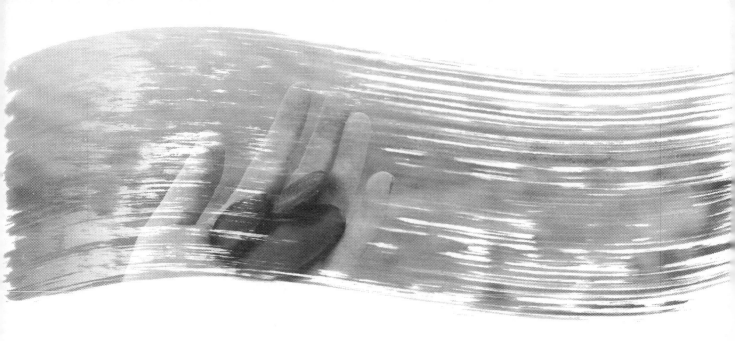

Spiritual Gifts Inventory & Reflection Guide

❑ Complete the Spiritual Gifts Survey provided in this lesson. Or use the online tool at **SpiritualGiftsTest.com**.

❑ Use the chart below to record your results and write out a description next to each gift.

❑ Sit quietly.

❑ Pray.

❑ Ask the Holy Spirit to help you *see* these gifts and how to invest in using them in your day-to-day life.

❑ Begin looking for clues to understand more clearly your God-given purpose and vision.

Spiritual Gift	Description	How I can invest in using this gift in my day-to-day life.

Spiritual Gifts Inventory Reflection Questions

Take some time to read over the answers you have written down in the boxes of the *Spiritual Gifts Inventory & Reflection Guide*. Pray, asking the Holy Spirit to help you discern and understand your spiritual gifts and how you can begin investing in using each in your day-to-day life, as well as in your future.

Then set a timer for 10–15 minutes, and record answers to some of the questions below:

God desires for us to *Go & See* how what we have can meet the needs of the "multitudes" when he miraculously multiplies the little bit we have.
Mark 6:30-44

1. What surprised you about the results of your Spiritual Gifts Survey results?
2. Did your results change your perspective of yourself? Why or how?
3. Which spiritual gifts do you think you least understand the definition and/or application of? What questions do you have about these gifts' purpose/application in your life?
4. Which spiritual gifts have you already seen yourself investing in using in daily life? Describe how you have used them.
5. Based on your spiritual gifts, what do you imagine you will do in the future to use these gifts in ministry, your career, or day-to-day life?

Processing Your Personality Type Grid

1. If you don't already know your Myers-Briggs personality type, head over to the 16personalities.com site to take the Personality Test. Understanding how you make decisions, learn, and recharge can bring you a fresh perspective and help you understand how you were built for impact in particular ways.

2. After you know your four-letter personality type, then find your personality type description in the Discipleship Guide for the 16 Myers-Briggs Personality Types (*Type this title into Google and it will take you to the jesusfilm.org site to download it.*). As you are reading, highlight insights that resonate with you.

3. Now, using the grid below, reflect on the ways the information connects with your spiritual gifts and your experiences in life so far. Record your insights, and look for patterns.

The 4-Letters that describe my personality traits are:	The name given for my personality type online is:	The name given for my personality type in the Become Like Jesus While Being Yourself Guide is:
_____	_____	_____

Spiritual Gifts	Personality Type	Your Life Experiences
List your top 3 or more if you have a tie. Record parts of the descriptions of the gift that resonate with you.	Record the descriptions about your personality traits (4 areas) that resonated with you.	Record memories that support/ affirm your spiritual gifts and the traits of your personality. **More hints:** special memories of delight, answered prayer, or seeing God use you to minister to someone or accomplish a task …
	(**I**ntrovert or **E**xtrovert)	
	(**S**ensing or i**N**tuitive)	
	(**T**hinking or **F**eeling)	
	(**J**udging or **P**erceiving)	

Notes:

Your Unique Design Artifact

Pray, reflect, and record on one page your discoveries from this chapter. This could be in paragraph or bullet form. Or you could get creative and use a graphic organizer or pictures. The goal is for you to create an artifact that helps you to see the "two fish and five loaves" (Mark 6:38) and the "talents" (Matthew 25:14–30) given to you by your Master to invest continually until his return.

Set a timer for 30–45 minutes, and get to work.

> The Exclusive Combination of Natural Talents, Spiritual Gifts, and
> Personality Traits Assigned Specifically to Me to Enjoy & Invest

Lesson: 6

Relationships are Gifts and Guides

Purpose and Context

God desires for us to Go & See how what we have can meet the needs of the "multitudes" when he miraculously multiplies the little bit we have.

Mark 6:30-44

We have all been given talents that we are asked to invest [multiply] until the day our master returns and asks us to give an account for what we did with what he gave us.

Matthew 25:14-30

We are forgetful. Thus, we need to set-up "stones of remembrance" as markers of God's faithfulness, strength and involvement in our journey.

Joshua 4

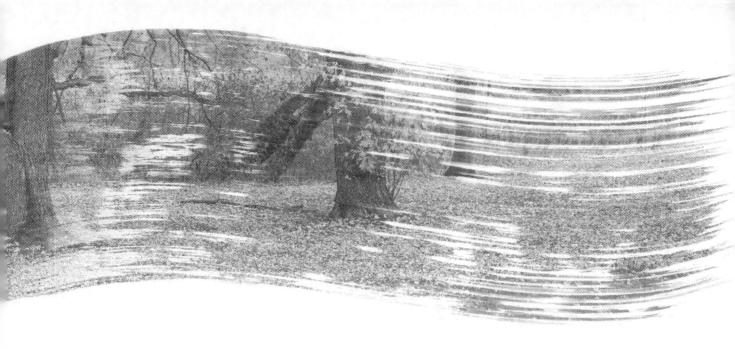

Introduction

Throughout the last five lessons of this study, you have taken time to consider how the following guide you toward understanding and living out your purpose and vision: the stories and parables from the Bible, your personal history, and your unique design (*natural talents, spiritual gifts, and personality traits*). Yet there is one more aspect of your life that needs examining and diagramming in order for you to fully comprehend one of the most essential elements of your purpose and vision—*relationships*.

From the beginning of time it has been this relational component of our being that sets us apart from all other created things. Our internal desire and need for relationships was set into us by a God who "created mankind in his image" (Genesis 1:27) by breathing his spirit into Adam and then into Eve. In Eden humanity and God walked together, living in relationship with one another. Our design from the start was intended to be in "helpmate" relationships with others and a "walking day-to-day" relationship with God (Genesis 2:18–25 Darby).

Even though the Fall wrecked the natural ability for these relationships to flourish, the purpose and vision of our design is unchanged. We were made for one another. We were made in the image of a relationship-focused God who operates out of an everlasting triune relationship—Father, Son, and Holy Spirit. Thus, taking inventory of our relationships, understanding the impact they have had on us, and then setting forth to invest our "talents" by investing in relationships with others is not optional. Rather, it is fundamental to living out the purpose we have been set in this time and place to fulfill.

Everything in our being is oriented toward relationship, with God and others. Yet, for most of us, relationships can be one of the greatest sources of challenge, frustration, and disappointment. However, the level of challenge found in growing and maintaining healthy relationships does not give us permission to dismiss the importance, necessity, and significance of God's design for us to live in relationship with one another. In fact, the challenges should signal to us the need to pull on the armor of God and fight for the

We have all been given talents that we are asked to invest [multiply] until the day our master returns and asks us to give an account for what we did with what he gave us.

Matthew 25:14-30

relationships given to us by the God who chose to set each of us at this specific time in history and in our specific locations geographically—all for a divine and holy purpose.

All the people in your life are known to God. All the relationships in your life are known to God. Believe that. Let it propel you toward choosing to *Go & See* how each relationship in your past and present is guiding you toward knowing and living out your purpose and vision. Consider thinking of relationships in this way: each relationship is an endowment you have been given to invest in while the master is away (Matthew 25:14–28). Each relationship abounds with opportunities to invite Jesus into multiplying your "loaves and fishes" to meet the needs of those around you (Mark 6:38–39). Each relationship is a precious gift. Let that lens guide your reflections and prayers as you walk through this session.

 ## Reflection & Application

Throughout my life I have been overwhelmingly blessed with family, teachers, coaches, and colleagues who inspire me and push me toward goals I wouldn't likely have worked toward had I not known each of them. First, let's start with the past. I grew up in a small town of less than a thousand people. My visits to my hometown are infrequent to say the least. Thus, interactions with people from my upbringing are sparse. Yet there is a deep well of gratitude and appreciation in my heart and soul for the ways the adults from that time in my life helped me become who I am today. As a result, I have determined that whenever I have the opportunity to honor these people and thank them for how they shaped me, I will seize it.

Several months ago I ran into my high school track coach. We have kept up some over the years. As our conversation unfolded that day, I knew this was an opportunity to be seized. So, as awkward as it felt, I let words of gratitude and appreciation leave my heart through my mouth. His response caught me off guard. He looked me straight in the eyes and said, "You need to always remember that impact goes both ways. Your life has impacted mine more than you will ever know."

I was at a literal loss for words, as I tried hard to not appear choked up and teary-eyed. What I had just heard was something I had never in my thirty-six years of life considered: The way I was living was impacting people older than me. The testimony of what I did as a teen and then as an adult has brought courage and change to the people who raised me. How could it be?

Yet this is the truth. Impact works both ways. Even though my motivation in the above conversation was to express my gratitude, I was gifted with a word of encouragement and a reminder that all the relationships in our lives are designed to provide strength to one another. And isn't this what the second greatest commandment is all about?

"Teacher, which is the greatest commandment in the Law?"

Jesus replied: "'Love the Lord your God with all your heart and with all your soul and with all your mind. This is the first and greatest commandment. And the second is like it: 'Love your neighbor as yourself.' All the Law and the Prophets hang on these two commandments." (Matthew 22:36–40)

We absolutely cannot live out the second greatest commandment if we are not in relationship with others. One of the ways I feel most loved is when I am affirmed and encouraged by the sincere words of another. Words not about specific accomplishments but ones that affirm that my unique design is recognized. Words that reveal my life isn't invisible. Words that confirm that how I am living is pointing others to love, grace, and freedom. Words of life.

We are forgetful. Thus, we need to set up "stones of remembrance" as markers of God's faithfulness, strength and involvement in our journey.
Joshua 4

These are the words that I want to encourage others with as well. But I can't get there unless I am living in sincere, honest, and loyal relationships with others. In addition, I can't see how others are building me up and *fanning my flame* (2 Timothy 1:6) if I don't stop and reflect on **who** God has set in my path to guide me, build me up, and provide me with opportunities to live out my purpose and vision.

Experts say the first step in overcoming a bad habit is admitting you have one. I believe that can be turned around a bit and applied here: to **see the gift** that relationships are in molding and guiding you toward using your natural and spiritual gifts (i.e., living your purpose and vision), the first step is admitting those relationships exist. The next step is listing each and defining the impact. Which is then followed by seizing every opportunity to express gratitude and affirmation for the gifts these relationships have increased or matured in you.

Now it is time to get to work. Pull out your journal and get to a quiet place of mind. It is time to *Go & See* the ways relationships have been both a gift and guide in your life. The relationships of our formative years are highly impactful but often get set aside and forgotten until we intentionally summon them to the surface. Let your mind walk back to some of your earliest relationships first. After you've sat in quiet reflection for several minutes, begin answering each of the questions below as fully as possible.

Check off each one as you *go*.

- ☐ **1)** At the top of the page, write this title, **My Faith Lineage**. Then start making a list of all the people who have helped you know yourself or Jesus better.
- ☐ **2)** How could recognizing and recording your faith lineage (*the people who have shaped your life and faith*) have an impact on you and/or those around you?
- ☐ **3)** What relationships has God used to unlock something in you that turned out to be crucial in increasing your "talents" (*natural or spiritual gifts*)?
- ☐ **4)** Who has God used to grow you in your courage to obey him or affirmed you in your purpose or vision? How did they do this for you?

Notes:

Digging Deeper

This lesson asks you to consider your spiritual and natural heritages and the impact each has on your present and future. In addition, you will be asked to recognize and begin to plan for the legacy you desire to leave by the ways you choose to live and **invest what you have been given** now and in the future.

To get started on this journey of placing relationships in our minds as gifts and guides to understanding our purpose and vision, let's *Go & See* what the Bible reveals on this concept. *Go* grab your Bible and read 2 Timothy 1. Highlight the verses that stick out to you.

Did you *see* the following?

- Paul affirms Timothy's faith, not based on Timothy's actions but with a reminder to Timothy of the sincere faith Timothy's grandmother and mother passed on to him.
- Paul reminds Timothy that the "flame" of the gift of God is on him, not because of anything he accomplished, but by the "laying on of my hands" and the power of the Spirit.
- "Guard the good deposit that was entrusted to *you*—guard it with the help of the Holy Spirit who lives in *us*" (verse 14, italics added).
  - Singular pronoun (*you*) – individual assignment
  - Plural pronoun (*us*) – collective power and purpose

A bit of context to get us started: In the book of 2 Timothy, the apostle Paul is writing from prison to his disciple Timothy. It is important to note that Paul opens with words of encouragement and affirmation to his "son" in the faith, Timothy. In addition, Paul calls into recognition Timothy's heritage and the role it plays in his calling (future assignments). Paul is building Timothy up through a very sincere recognition of the impact Timothy's faith and perseverance has had on Paul's faith. (Remember, impact works both ways.)

Second, Paul points Timothy back to the faith heritage from which he has come. Both of these forms of affirmation stem from the relationships that Timothy can look to when he needs evidence of the Spirit living in him. One is biological, and the other is not. Yet both are able to aid Timothy in continuing to confidently spread the "flame" of the gospel to others. In other words, our spiritual heritage and familial relationships are to light our way and give us courage and hope to persevere in our purpose and vision.

The relationship between Paul and Timothy reveals that a person's spiritual heritage may not be built from those who are genetically members of their family tree. Likewise, one's legacy may extend beyond biological or familial relationships. This is because, in Christ, we are all one family—all adopted sons and daughters, heirs to the kingdom (Ephesians 1:5).

Our mission here on earth is to help one another get to heaven having obeyed all that God has commanded us to do. The writer of Hebrews likens this obedience to running a race. Just as a runner takes no possessions along on a run, our race of faith requires us to set everything down that hinders us and focus on who is running with us and where we are going. We can take nothing with us from this world, except people. Hence the need to truly know how to invest in relationships while we have breath in our lungs.

The book of Psalms also provides encouragement and instruction on the necessity of knowing and recording our faith lineage. Take a few minutes to *Go & See* what is written in Psalm 78:1–11.

Did you *see* this?

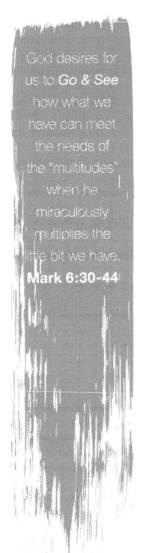

God desires for us to **Go & See** how what we have can meet the needs of the "multitudes" when he miraculously multiplies the little bit we have.
Mark 6:30-44

- The people take ownership of passing on the good deeds of the Lord, his power and wonders, to the next generation.
- The people profess that the forefathers are commanded to teach their children the promises and commands of God—so that the next generation will teach the following generation.
- We are to remember and share with the next generation the work of God in our lives, to instruct them on living in His presence, and help them see that following His purposes provides protection from destruction (see verses 8–11 ESV).

In this psalm we see yet another reason to recognize, record, and share stories about the relationships that have built our faith, gifts, purpose, and vision. Namely, so that the next generation will know God. Just as the stones set up in Joshua 4 were to be a testimony to future generations, taking the time to record our faith story and the lineage of our faith, we can lead our children (biological or spiritual) to a steady faith—one built on understanding their unique design, purpose, and vision for their generation.

We want the next generation to profess and build their own faith and relationship with God, but we need to recognize that the roots of their growth begin with the relationship we have with them. So too for us. Our faith might be our own, but we were molded, equipped, and guided by those who have gone before us. In order for your mind and soul to fully grasp this, to move it from abstract to concrete, writing it down or drawing it out will likely be necessary.

Another reason making a record of your faith lineage is important is that as you start leading others, it can be easy to forget the relationships that led you to where you are. Fighting to remember how the "flames" got started in your faith and sharing those stories with others is important and impactful because it "fans the flame" in your soul and the souls of those who hear it.

Why?

Because it reminds you that you didn't get to where you are on your own. Keeping in mind that you are on a collective (not an individual) journey will likely propel you to pass on the same gift to others. And just like the stones set up in Joshua 4, your life and stories of God's faithfulness can become hallmarks that others see and cue them to remember God's sovereignty and saving grace.

Tool 6: Family Tree of Faith

Family Tree of Faith: Recalling key people and recording your lineage of faith. The aim of this activity is for you to create an image or artifact that reflects the ways God has used relationships to grow and guide you.

Recognizing the specific people within your spiritual lineage—both what you receive and what you pass down—is incredibly beneficial to your faith journey. Additionally, this tool can illuminate for your soul God's sovereignty over the relationships in your life, producing joy, thanks, and praise for your Creator. Finally, recording your lineage of faith in image form is another way to set up *stones of remembrance* so that the generations to come can *Go & See* the work and blessings of God in your life and on the earth.

Instructions

1. Using the Faith Family Tree Brainstorming and Prewriting page, begin making a record of the relationships that have been gifts and guides to you.
2. Using the Faith Family Tree page, create an image of your **Family Tree of Faith**. (There is a template you can use if drawing isn't one of your delights—and a sketch of My Faith Family Tree at the end of the lesson, to give you some ideas.)
3. Now it's time to put your brave on and practice passing on the story of God's faithfulness to the "next" generation. *Go* and share your **Faith Family Tree** with your child, spouse, parent, youth pastor, or mentor or with a friend or extended family member.

The Next Step

Do you remember the story I shared at the opening of this lesson? The one about my high school track coach and my impromptu awkward words of gratitude that were met with encouragement that changed my perspective on impact. From this story we saw that gratitude is a powerful action that we can take to encourage and build one another up—which all of us are called to do within the body of Christ (1 Thessalonians 5:11). However, the press for efficiency and the cultural acceptance of living busy lives sometimes gets in the way of taking the time to write or speak words of gratitude to the people who have built us up.

Like me, perhaps you'd rather wait for an impromptu meeting to muster up some unpolished words of gratitude. But completing a **Faith Family Tree the Next Step Planner** can help you express gratitude more frequently and intentionally. First, make a list of the names on your **Faith Family Tree**. Then search out each person's mailing or email address and record it next to each person's name. Then next to each name give yourself a date by which you will contact that person to express your gratitude for the ways he or she has impacted your life. Then write a letter (or email) to each one prior to the deadline you listed next to his or her name.

If you are struggling to know what to write, ask the Holy Spirit to guide you. The number of words doesn't matter. Sincerity, encouragement, and gratitude are the goals. The more specific you can be about what impacted you, the clearer your message of gratitude will be. However, a short written and sent letter is better than no letter. So don't get hung up on making it perfect.

Once your letter is complete, don't forget to mail or deliver it.

Closing

The pursuit of understanding our gifts is a battle. It is a battle to intentionally seek depth in relationships. It is a battle to believe that the effectiveness of the parts of the body of Christ hinges on each part's connectedness to Christ and to one another. But we all have the tools we need for battle:

- Christ's atoning blood that washes our conscience clear,
- the Holy Spirit who illuminates our purpose and the relationships around us that tangibly tether us together, and
- A united mission, which is to display God's glory, his love, and his active involvement in the little corner of the earth we find our two feet planted in for now.

Yet investing in relationships may prove to be much easier said than done. Relationships are hard work. Our failures and the failures of others can trip us up on our race to the finish line. However, we are given all we need, through Christ, to not let the pratfalls leave us on the ground for long.

Of late, through conversations and words that have been somewhat like boxing blows to the side, I have come to a new dependence on and understanding of grace. *Grace* is such an eloquent and beautiful word. But it came at such a brutal cost—bloodshed and death.

Grace from heaven is freely given, and I delight in the grace I receive. But to extend grace is a constant and exhausting wrestling match that takes place in my heart, mind, and soul. To be grace to the ones who jab my sides is a brutal fight. A fight that cost a death; grace required Christ's death. And for grace to win in my heart, a death must come to my desires to seek truth and justice for selfish gain or emotional satisfaction.

Grace has already won me. But to allow grace to win in me, the full armor of God must be put on. I must suit up and fight to believe that I win, the church wins, and relationship wins when I set aside my defenses and let grace truly cover the offenses.

Why?

Because grace makes way for forgiveness. Forgiveness ushers in freedom—glorious, undeserved freedom!

Freedom releases us from pain, bondage, and mind games. Grace, forgiveness, and freedom keep relationships intact and the body of Christ effective. And this is why relationships increase our Christlikeness, propel us toward our purpose, and build up lineage after lineage of faith.

Ask the Holy Spirit to reveal to you more clearly all the ways he has entrusted the gifts of relationships to you to love God more completely and love his people more intentionally. Pray for discernment to know in what area(s) of your life you need to intentionally pursue deeper relationships with others—for example, friends, neighbors, co-workers, mentors, parents, children, those who don't know God yet, widows, orphans, or the elderly.

Pray that you will know what obedience looks like for you and that you would know how to access the power, resources, and creativity to obey. Take one step, and then the next one, and the next. Soon each step will be just a little bit easier. Or you'll be stronger, so it will at least seem easier.

Jesus once said to his disciples, "Your love for one another will prove to the world that you are my disciples" (John 13:35 NLT). How we live in relationship with others impacts the world of observers around us. Take the time often to *Go & See* who has helped prove to you, through the way he or she loved, that relationships graft us into a tree of faith that started with the lineage of Jesus. Reminisce about those dear ones who loved you unconditionally, with grace and truth, setting you on the path you are on today. Let your remembering and documenting fill you with a gratitude that motivates you to keep the faith family tree growing.

Go & See.

Faith Family Tree Brainstorming & Prewriting

1. Set a timer for 10 minutes. Use the entire time to work on the two lists below. Brainstorm by writing down anything and everything that comes to mind.

   ☐ **List 1**: Make a list of your spiritual gifts, natural talents, and delights.
   ☐ **List 2:** Make a list of words that describe: who you are, what makes you *you*, your personality traits, or any words that describe how you relate to Christ and others.

2. Now next to each of the things on your lists, write the names of people or types of relationships that created or fostered those things in your life.

List 1		List 2	
Step One	**Step Two**	**Step One**	**Step Two**
Gifts, Talents, or Delights	Person/People of impact/influence	Character traits & Personality	Person/People of impact/influence

My Faith Family Tree

Using the names you generated on the **Faith Family Tree Brainstorming & Prewriting** page, create an image that reflects the names of the people you added to your lists. This could be adding names to your timeline, or it could be making a new drawing. Work with your delights and gifts to create something that you can return to and *see* the path of God's purpose and visions coming to life through the people he has set into your path. (*There is a template on the next page you can use if drawing is not your delight.*)

Family Tree

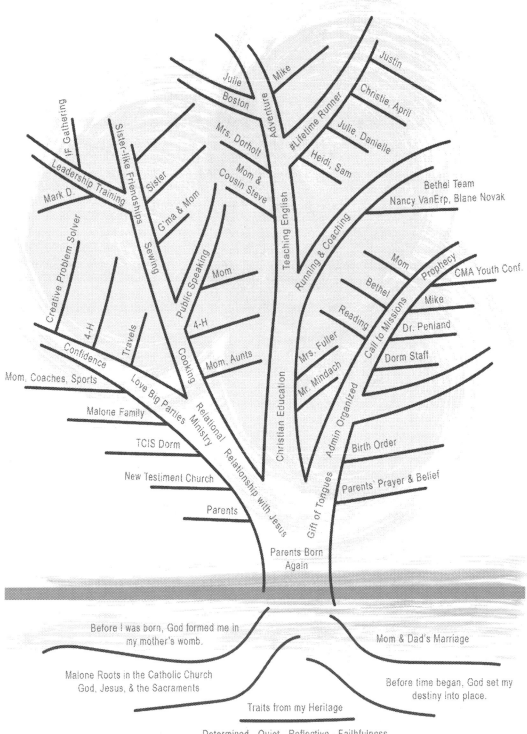

Julie
Mike
Justin
Boston
Christie, April
Julie, Danielle
Mrs. Dorholt
Heidi, Sam
Adventure
#Lifetime Runner
iF Gathering
Sister-like Friendships
Sister
Mom & Cousin Steve
Bethel Team
Nancy VanErp, Blane Novak
Leadership Training
G'ma & Mom
Teaching English
Mark D.
Running & Coaching
Mom
Prophecy
CMA Youth Conf.
Creative Problem Solver
Public Speaking
Bethel
Mike
Mom
Reading
Dr. Penland
4-H
Call to Missions
4-H
Travels
Cooking
Mom, Aunts
Mrs. Fuller
Dorm Staff
Confidence
Mr. Mindach
Mom, Coaches, Sports
Love Big Parties
Relational Ministry
Christian Education
Admin Organized
Malone Family
Birth Order
TCIS Dorm
Relationship with Jesus
New Testament Church
Gift of Tongues
Parents' Prayer & Belief
Parents

Parents Born Again

Before I was born, God formed me in my mother's womb.

Mom & Dad's Marriage

Malone Roots in the Catholic Church
God, Jesus, & the Sacraments

Before time began, God set my destiny into place.

Traits from my Heritage

Determined - Quiet - Reflective - Faithfulness

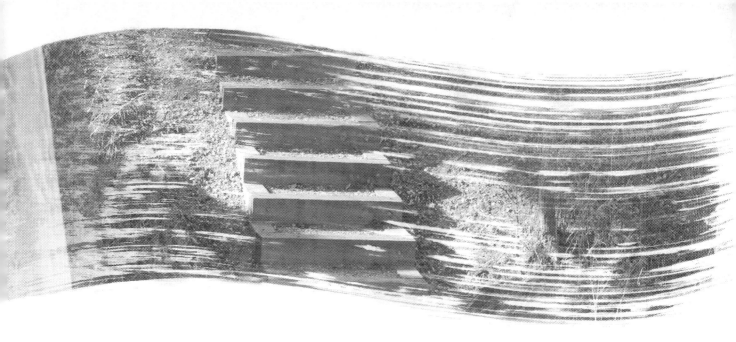

Faith Family Tree – The Next Step Planner

1. Make a list of the names on your **Faith Family Tree**.
2. Find each person's mailing or email address
3. Next to each name give yourself a date by which you will contact that person to express your gratitude for the ways he or she has impacted your life.
4. Write a letter or email to each person.
5. Once your letter is complete, don't forget to mail or deliver the letter.

Person's Name	Mailing or Email Address	Goal Date for Sending Letter	Checkmark here when Completed

Notes:

Notes:

Lesson: 7

Investing in Relationships Requires Planning

Go & See

Purpose and Context

God desires for us to Go & See how what we have can meet the needs of the "multitudes" when he miraculously multiplies the little bit we have.
Mark 6:30-44

We have all been given talents that we are asked to invest [multiply] until the day our master returns and asks us to give an account for what we did with what he gave us.
Matthew 25:14-30

We are forgetful. Thus, we need to set-up "stones of remembrance" as markers of God's faithfulness, strength and involvement in our journey.
Joshua 4

Introduction

In Lesson 6, Relationships are Gifts and Guides, we took the time to consider and examine how it's *not optional* to take inventory of our relationships, understand the impact they have had on us, and then set forth to invest our lives by investing in relationships with others. Instead, it's fundamental to living out the role we have been designed to fulfill throughout this one life we get to live here on earth. We also looked at the significance and impact of believing that we are made in the image of a relationship-centered God. Then you walked through the steps of recalling key people in your life and creating a Faith Family Tree to reflect the ways God has used relationships to grow and guide you.

In Lesson 6, most of your time was spent looking back to reflect on and record those people who have built your faith, gifts, talents, or personality traits or your courage to run after your dreams. In doing so, I pray that your reflections led to increased honor and gratitude for those who have been instrumental in you becoming who you are today. In this lesson, you are going to turn your reflective eyes forward and use them to create a vision of your future in regard to the variety of relationships you need to flourish and serve others.

Loving God is hard work. Sometimes loving people is even harder work. A famous army officer once said that failing to plan is planning to fail. This is just as true in relationships as it is in any other area of our life. Thus, the objective of this lesson is to help you make a plan for investing in the lives of others. I pray this verse encourages you throughout your process: "May the God who gives endurance and encouragement give you the same attitude of mind toward each other that Christ Jesus had, so that with one mind and one voice you may glorify the God and Father of our Lord Jesus Christ" (Romans 15:5–6).

We have all been given talents that we are asked to invest [multiply] until the day our master returns and asks us to give an account for what we did with what he gave us.
Matthew 25:14-30

Reflection & Application

We need people. For real. This is a human and a spiritual need. As much as American culture tries to hold up the self-made man as the role model for success, I believe that deep in our souls we know that to be self-made and successful on our own, without the help of others, actually leaves us lonely, confused, and quite frankly living a lie. Instead, the phrase *no man is an island* (from a John Donne sermon in the seventeenth century) is closer to the truth—both the truth as we experience in reality, and also the truth we are called to biblically. Donne writes:

> No man is an island, entire of itself; every man is a piece of the continent, a part of the main; if a clod [lump of earth] be washed away by the sea, Europe is the less, as well as if a promontory [a headland] were, as well as if a manor [an estate] of thy friend's or of thine own were; any man's death diminishes me, because I am involved in mankind, and therefore never send to know for whom the bell tolls; it tolls for thee. (*Devotions Upon Emergent Occasions,* John Donne)

As Christians, single members that make up one body in Christ, our marching orders stand in contrast to many of the habits and patterns of thinking in American culture. This is because the American mind-set of ambition and focus on individualism, efficiency, and consumerism often trumps relationships and loyalty. In contrast, as Christians, we are called to live out the belief that we need one another in order to live out the truths of our professed allegiance to Christ. This may require setting aside self-focused achievements, and taking up a teammate perspective (to do so might decrease one's efficiency) and quite possibly require setting aside success, as the world defines it. Ultimately, we are to counterculture by placing a higher value on relationships and the Great Commission than on possessions, success, or personal preferences.

Not only do we need relationships, but we also grow best when those relationships come in a variety of forms. We need all kinds of voices and people in our lives to help us run our race well: mentors, shepherds, friends, running buddies, prayer warriors, and observers. Some of these people fall into the routine of our lives, and we can easily make time for them. Others cross our paths now and then but not without effort and intentionality. Though we would all love to be the ones invited into intentional, deep relationships, it isn't a practical way to think or live. If everyone is waiting around to be the one invited, no one will be doing the inviting. Most important, impactful relationships won't just happen. They will likely require planning, follow-through, and courage.

In addition, just as you need others, *others need you*. Recognizing that others need you is paramount to taking hold of living the call to purposeful relationships commissioned to each of us by our Creator. In a world full of messages that encourage selfishness, it is easy to dismiss "other people need me" as just a phrase. However, in reality, building such relationships becomes an act of selflessness when this concept is approached from humility and with a mind and heart that says, *"Others just might need my words of encouragement to keep persevering. If I hold back from believing others need me to serve and encourage them in their faith, I could be holding them back from using their gifts."*

Pull out your journal and get to a quiet place of mind. *Go & See* what the Holy Spirit is revealing to you about your need for relationship and others' need for you. Answer each question as fully as possible. Check off each one as you *go*.

God desires for us to *Go & See* how what we have can meet the needs of the "multitudes" when he miraculously multiplies the little bit we have. **Mark 6:30-44**

- ☐ **1)** How have people in your life helped you persevere or grow in the assignments or purpose set in front of you in this season of life?
- ☐ **2)** Is there a type of person (mentor, pastor, friend, prayer warrior, running buddy) that is missing in your life right now?
  - ☐ **a)** If so, describe the role that is missing and why you are in need of it.
- ☐ **3)** Do you believe others need you in order to persevere, grow, or be set free?
  - ☐ **a)** Who comes to mind when you consider who may need you in any of these ways?
- ☐ **4)** What might be holding you back from using your words or actions to be what another person needs in order to persevere, grow, or be set free?
- ☐ **5)** What is the danger in believing the lie that no one needs you or that your life is not impacting others?

Notes:

Digging Deeper

Pinning our beliefs and actions to specific truths found in passages of the Bible is essential to remaining in line with the promises and commands of God. Let's *Go & See* what the Bible says about our need for others, their need for us, and the world's need for all the members of the body of Christ to be actively investing in relationships.

Grab your Bible and read the following passages, highlighting the verses or words that stick out to you as *instructions on the need for and role of relationships in a Christian's life.*

- ❑ Exodus 20:1–17
- ❑ Mark 12:28–34
- ❑ Colossians 3:12–15
- ❑ 1 Thessalonians 5:11

If you grew up in church, you likely had to memorize the Ten Commandments, found in Exodus 20:1–17. The commands given to Moses begin with laws that show us how to have a *right relationship with God* and end with laws that show us how to have a *right relationship with others.* Don't miss the significance of this. Healthy relationships with others begin with a healthy relationship with God. And building healthy relationships with others is paramount to obeying God and living into his promises.

When was the last time you went back and looked at the Ten Commandments, reflected on them, or asked yourself if your actions and words most often demonstrate obedience to God in these areas?

Grace certainly covers for our shortcomings, and Christ's death on the cross means salvation comes through belief in him, not living a perfect life. Yet obedience to these commands hasn't been dismissed. This is hard work. We won't nail it every day. But our goal is to keep working always in the direction of holiness and obedience. It is important to notice that six (*a majority*) of the commandments instruct us on right relationships with others (*all four of the other commands concern our relationship with God*). In short, we cannot obey God without choosing to build relationships that show honor, respect, and obedience to the Ten Commandments.

This concept of obedience in relationships to others as a pathway to obedience to God is also found in Mark 12:26–34 and Colossians 3:12–15. In both of these passages we *see* that we cannot follow the "greatest" or the "second greatest" commandment if we are not living in relationship with God and others. Again we *see* clearly: we need to live self-sacrificial, loving relationships with people in order to obey God.

In even better news, we are not ill equipped to do so. Love, through Christ and the power of the Holy Spirit, is continually being poured into us in order that we are able to fulfill these commands in all of our relationships. Not only that, but this Christ-powered love is our source of strength for remaining resolute in both beginning and maintaining relationships.

We must always remember, we exist for God and for those who need God. Both the Old and New Testaments show us this. Furthermore, Christ came to give us the grace, power, and tools to live out this divine purpose every day we are breathing on this side of heaven.

The most practical place to start with living a life of actively investing in relationships that meet needs and spur others on toward love and good deeds is with our words. First Thessalonians 5:11 helps us *see* that encouragement is how we build one another up because it brings out strength in people. Encouragement, though often done with words, can come in many forms:

- What you give (Mark 12:41–44).
- What you say (Proverbs 16:24).
- What you do (Matthew 25).
- How you choose to live (Ephesians 5:1–2).

We are designed to spur one another on toward love and good deeds. We are called to live from a posture of humility so starkly different from the world's point of view that it stops people in their tracks and causes them to wonder what makes us different. We are made with a purpose to maintain relationships within the body that are so harmonious that the world will look at us and know love and *see* that our identity as followers of Christ impacts how we do relationships.

But how do we do this when it seems that everything in this fallen world aims to hinder the building up of healthy relationships?

How do we do this when relationships can also be a source of pain, discouragement, and brokenness?

By determining to let our hearts, minds, and souls be conformed to the mind of Christ. We do this by combing through God's truths, commands, and promises in the Bible on a regular and consistent basis—looking specifically for passages that remind us that "no man is an island" and those that direct us on how to live as if we authentically believe all that the Bible teaches is true and good for us. In addition, we can live a relationship-focused life by inviting the Holy Spirit in to provide the power to take every negative or unproductive thought captive in order to **choose to believe the best** of those around us. Lastly, we must not forget that investing in relationships requires discipline and intentionality—neither of which is likely to come naturally or easily.

To sum up, it takes perseverance and humility to invite others into our lives with the specific intention of asking them to spur us on. Yet finding just one person to be the sole source of your spurring isn't the goal. This is for many reasons, but one of them is that God has given us an entire body of voices to help guide us. Conversely, for the same reasons, we shouldn't be another person's sole source of spurring.

If we believe there is a God who sets us in our specific time and place and divinely sets our steps to cross the paths of those around us, then we can believe that making a plan to invest in those relationships is honoring God and is living out our purpose. Yet it is pretty easy to live as though we believe our interactions are accidental or random. Let's choose to run from that lie by taking inventory of the relationships God has provided for us and then making a plan to intentionally invest in those relationships, even when it gets hard and complicated.

Tool 7: Relationship Investment Plan

Relationship Investment Plan: Creating a plan to invest your time and gifts in building relationships with others.

Our lives are meant to spur others on toward love and good deeds—not as an option but as a need. Spurring others on and meeting their needs don't usually happen naturally. Yes, we may find ourselves in relationships no matter what, but it takes the Holy Spirit, discipline, and intentionality to foster relationships that spur others on.

It is important to recognize that we need to have relationships with those who can easily relate to our season of life, but we also need people who have gone before us as well as some who are a season or two behind. We need people who are full of affirmation for what they *see* in us. Additionally, these affirming voices should be balanced by people who are courageous enough to help us *see* gaps or nearsightedness in our thinking or inconsistencies in our behaviors.

As noted earlier in this lesson, it is important to remember that there is a danger in believing the lie that no one needs you or that your life is not impacting others. *Seeing* the truth of your life's impact, and committing to growing more consistent in your intentionality toward investing in others who need your encouraging words or who need to *see* the example of life that you live, will likely grow you in ways you can't even envision completely right now. But by faith, we move toward the little bit we can *see*, trusting that God will continue to guide our steps as we move forward under his sovereignty.

This tool, **Relationship Investment Plan**, is designed to allow you to take inventory of the people in your life right now and examine whether some types of voices are missing in your relationships. It then aids you in making a plan to intentionally create time and space to invest in one or more relationships that you need. Lastly, you will use this tool to outline the ways you can begin to intentionally invest in relationships that build others up through spurring them on or meeting a need by using what you have been given: life experiences, natural talents, spiritual gifts, personality traits, relationships, and grace.

 ## Instructions

1. Complete **Section 1: Who is in your life now?** on the ***Relationship Investment Plan***. This section is designed to help you take inventory of the people in your life right now and examine if certain types of voices are missing.
2. Complete **Section 2: Who You Need Action Plan**, on the ***Relationship Investment Plan***. This section provides instructions on making a plan for intentionally creating time and space to invest in those relationships that you are in need of (*filling in any gaps you noted from Section 1*).
3. Complete **Section 3: Who needs you now?** on the ***Relationship Investment Plan***. This section is designed to help you take inventory of the people you are actively investing in now.
4. Complete **Section 4: Who Needs You – Action Plan**, on the ***Relationship Investment Plan***. This section provides instructions on making a plan for intentionally creating time and space to invest in those people who need you (*filling in any gaps you noted from Section 3*).

 ## The Next Step

Congratulations! Your hard work and focus have gotten you through seven lessons on using tools to excavate and articulate all the "talents" you've been given to invest from now until the master returns or takes you home (Matthew 25:14–30). What you perhaps thought was just a couple of loaves of bread and two fish is likely to have miraculously multiplied simply through the actions of *Going & Seeing* what you already have. I hope that you are at least a little bit surprised by all that you have found and that in the weeks ahead your surprise will birth wonder, awe, and, most importantly, action toward living out your purpose, vision, and values.

Go back and read the passages this study opened with:

❑ Mark 6:30–44
❑ Matthew 25:14–30
❑ Joshua 4

For this lesson's *Next Step*, I want you to truly get away to a quiet place with this book and all your work in hand.

Here is a list of your artifacts to help you make sure you have gathered everything before setting off:

- ❏ timeline,
- ❏ cleaned stones,
- ❏ personal essay,
- ❏ faith family tree, and
- ❏ relationship investment plan

Set a timer for five minutes. Use this time to pause and invite the Holy Spirit in with a prayer or a song of worship. Then examine each artifact you have created. As you examine, give thanks.

Reset your timer for five more minutes. Use this time to reexamine your artifacts, using your imagination to *see* yourself as one of the disciples faced with a crowd of hungry people (Mark 6:30–44). Imagine that all your discoveries on the journey through this study are loaves and fish, like what the disciples found when Jesus said, "**Go and see what you have.**"

Now *see* yourself handing Jesus your "loaves and fish," believing that he is delighted you have brought them to him. Then *see* yourself watching him pray over what you have given him. See him begin to break your gifts into pieces in order to perform a miracle to feed the multitude.

Reset your timer for five more minutes. Use this time to re-examine your artifacts, engaging your imagination to *see* yourself as the tenant who was given five talents (Matthew 25:14–30). Imagine that all your discoveries on the journey through this study are the talents you have invested and *seen* grow. You are the servant who went away and invested all that she had while her master was away. You are the one who, upon the master's return, was told, "Well done, good and faithful servant! You have been faithful with a few things; I will put you in charge of many things. Come and share your master's happiness!" (25:21).

Then pray and ask for creativity, wisdom, and perseverance to live as though you believe you have the strength, power, and vision to be that tenant. Believe your master already knows he put you in just the right place, at just the right time, with just the right gifts to be his good and faithful servant. He *sees*. He hears. He delights in your destiny.

And when the crowd comes and interrupts your quiet, let them in. *See* them as the necessary catalyst for growing your faith, using your gifts, and ushering in God's miracles here on earth.

And who knows but that you have come to your royal position for such a time as this?
—Esther 4:14

Notes:

Closing

One's physical body needs all the parts to be active and responding to each other in order to be whole and healthy. So too with the members of the body of Christ. You are one of those parts. And there is only one of you who can perform the unique function God designed you for. You are the only one who can meet the needs of the church and the world in your specific places and relationships. I wonder if this is the harder truth to submit to believing and courageously living out—*others need you* in order to

- be encouraged,
- be spurred on in their faith, or
- simply feel as though they are not really an island.

If you do not believe this, then you will likely not find the courage to put these truths into action in your thinking and living.

Recognize that you—the words you speak and the model you set for others—are needed for the health of the whole community around you. This is a truth I think we are too easily tempted to ignore out of busyness, insecurity, or fear. And we need to stop ignoring and setting aside our gifts, talents, and relationships.

Why?

Because *people need us*. They need us to actively live out the belief that in Christ, our words and actions have the power to set people free. We have been set free to set others free! The Word became flesh so that we could use our words and lives to stir one another up toward love and good deeds, encouraging one another as the [last] Day draws near (Hebrews 10:24–25).

Relationship is a gift of strength we can give to all those around us. Let's be people who recognize our need for others, their need for us, and the world's need to see who our Father is through us. We have been designed and commissioned to change the world. It starts by investing in one relationship at a time. And it continues with believing that relationships are God's mission plan for us all.

Do you remember that little song about a candle you learned as a preschooler, "This Little Light of Mine"?

One lyric says, "Hide it under a bushel? No! I'm gonna let it shine." How many of us are hiding our light (*personal history, natural talents, spiritual gifts or purpose*) under a basket because we are unsure whether our light really matters in the world?

When we think of one little light under a bushel (*which by the way would start a fire; but I digress*), it can seem insignificant. However, when all those lights that are sitting under bushels instead come out and join together to be one big light for the world to see, I guarantee our Abba in heaven will look down with pleasure and delight. Correspondingly, those around us will look toward the light and start asking questions about how they can have some of that life-changing light too.

When we break down the metaphor of the little light, we find that the song is really saying, *This little life of mine, I am going to let it build up and encourage the people around me.* In other words, I am going to believe and live out with words and actions the truth that my life is designed for impact. This impact begins with relationships—investing in them one at a time.

Living out our relational purposes will not be as easy as singing a song or learning what to do to have relationships, but a God-designed restoration plan will unfold when our words and actions are driven by intentionality, perseverance, and an understanding that without relationships we cannot obey all that God has asked of us. *We love God well by loving others extraordinarily. All our gifts are to be invested in doing those two things.* The result, along the way and in the end, will be miracles, multiplication, and stories of God's strength and faithfulness being passed from generation to generation.

Go & See.

Make a plan.

Invest.

Repeat.

We are forgetful. Thus, we need to set up "stones of remembrance" as markers of God's faithfulness, strength and involvement in our journey.

Joshua 4

Relationship Investment Plan

This tool is designed to help you take inventory of the people in your life right now and examine whether some types of voices are missing. Where there are gaps, this tool provides instructions on how to plan for intentionally creating time and space to invest in those relationships that you are lacking in. Secondly, you will use this tool to outline the ways you can begin to intentionally invest in relationships that build up, spur on, and meet needs based on all that you've been given.

Section 1: Who is in your life now?

Take 10–15 minutes to answer each of the following questions with names and *reasons each name fits the answer*. Then write an estimated amount of time you spend investing in these relationships.

Who do you need?	Names & Reasons	An estimated amount of investing time (per week, month or year)
Who are your mission-minded, like-minded friends?		
Who are people who help you love God more?		
Who can you safely share your purpose and visions with?		
Who are your "older than me" (mentors) friends you go to for guidance and perspective?		

Section 2: Who You Need Action Plan

As you examine the names and the amount of time you spend investing in these relationships, are there any categories that are deficient? Or are there any relationships that need more time invested in them? If so, create a plan for what that will look like in the coming weeks, months, or year. Use the questions below to get you started on a plan that is specific, attainable, and time-bound.

1. The area in my life in which I am in need of more relationships or need to spend more time investing is:
(Choose the one that is most deficient.)

   ❏ Mission-minded, like-minded friends

   ❏ People who make me love God more

   ❏ People with whom I can safely share my soul and deepest thoughts

   ❏ People who can mentor and guide me and offer perspective

2. What is holding me back from spending time with people who fit in this category (from question 1)?
(Check the one that most applies.)

   ❏ I am not intentionally setting aside (scheduling) time to invest in the relationships in this category.

   ❏ I am not in a relationship with anyone who fits in this category.

   ❏ I don't know how to invite someone into my life to meet this need.

3. Which action step best fits with my answers from above?
(Choose one.)

   ❏ I need to *Go & See* where there is room in my life to invest more intentionally in a relationship I have presently.

   ❏ I need to *Go & See* who I can invite into a relationship that meets the need I have.

4. **My Action Plan:**

   ❏ The specific relationship (category of/name of person) I will invest in or pursue is:

   _____

   _____

   _____

❑ A reasonable amount of time I can spend investing in this relationship is (i.e., X number of times per week, month, or year):

_____

_____

_____

❑ The day of the week/month I can make available for this relationship is:

_____

_____

_____

❑ I will begin investing in this relationship by (date):

_____

_____

_____

❑ I will commit to investing in this relationship for this amount of time (i.e., six months, a year, or two years):

_____

_____

_____

Section 3: Who needs you now?

Take 10–15 minutes to answer each of the following questions with names and *reasons each name fits the answer.* Then write an estimated amount of time you spend investing in these relationships.

Who needs you?	Names & Reasons	An estimated amount of investment time
Who is seeing God through you?		
Who are you discipling?		
Who are people you know who don't know Jesus but know you?		

Section 4: Who Needs You Action Plan

As you examine the names and the amount of time you spend investing in these relationships, are there any categories that are deficient? Or are there any relationships that are needing more time spent investing in them? If so, create a plan for what that will look like in the coming weeks, months, or year. Use the questions below to get you started on a plan that is specific, attainable, and time-bound.

1. The area in my life in which I am not using my time to invest in others who need me is: (Choose the one that is most deficient.)

    ❑ People who see God through me

    ❑ People I am discipling

    ❑ People who don't know Jesus

2. What is holding me back from spending time with people who fit in this category (from question 1)?
(Check the one that most applies.)

❑ I am not intentionally setting aside (scheduling) time to invest in the relationships in this category.

❑ I am not in a relationship with anyone who fits in this category.

❑ I don't know how to invite someone into my life to meet this need.

3. Which action step best fits with my answers from above?
(Choose one.)

❑ I need to *Go & See* where there is room in my life to invest more intentionally in a relationship I have presently.

❑ I need to *Go & See* who I can invite into a relationship that meets the need she has.

4. My Action Plan:

❑ The specific relationship (category of or name of person) I will invest in or pursue is:

_____

_____

❑ A reasonable amount of time I can spend investing in this relationship is (i.e., X number of times per week, month, or year):

_____

_____

_____

❑ The day of the week/month I can make available for this relationship is:

_____

_____

❑ I will begin investing in this relationship by (date):

_____

_____

❑ I will commit to investing in this relationship for this amount of time (i.e., six months, a year, or two years):

_____

_____

_____

Section 5: Prayer

Write out a prayer asking God to provide you strength, endurance, and favor as you obey his call to invest in relationships with others. Open up to him about your fears. Open up to him about your visions. Ask him to show you how he has designed you and set your steps in place to be in a relationship with the people who need you and the ones you need.

_____

_____

_____

_____

_____

_____

_____

_____

_____

_____

_____

_____

_____

_____

_____

_____

_____

_____

_____

_____

_____

_____

_____

_____

_____

*Some portions of the charts above are adapted from the, _Restless Study_, by Jennie Allen

Lesson: 8

Articulating Purpose, Vision and Values

Go & See

Purpose and Context

God desires for us to Go & See how what we have can meet the needs of the "multitudes" when he miraculously multiplies the little bit we have.
Mark 6:30-44

We have all been given talents that we are asked to invest [multiply] until the day our master returns and asks us to give an account for what we did with what he gave us.
Matthew 25:14-30

We are forgetful. Thus, we need to set-up "stones of remembrance" as markers of God's faithfulness, strength and involvement in our journey.
Joshua 4

Introduction

This week you are going to take all your learning from the last seven lessons and synthesize it into three categories: purpose, vision, and values. You will reflect on the experiences of your life, the people who have influenced you, and your natural talents, spiritual gifts, and personality traits to seek understanding and clarity.

The goal in this lesson is for you to interpret how your unique design—*your natural talents, spiritual gifts, personality traits, relationships, and life experiences*—can be used to help you articulate the *purpose*, your *vision*, and the *values* you must hold to in order to keep living out both your purpose and vision.

We established in previous lessons that God designed every part of who you are, where you have been, where you are, and where you are going. In addition, he uses all things to bring you to his goodness of redemption and provides the grace needed for a changed perspective (Romans 8:28). This is so that you can live according to the purposes he destined you to--a destiny set in you even before you were born (Psalm 139).

Why?

Because when we live out of a true understanding of who we are, we find an eternal assurance that propels us to look toward heaven, rather than to our circumstances, to discern our purpose in our time in history and the places our feet are set to travel each day.

It is worth noting, so that you can persevere through doubt and discouragements, that the path to living out your God-given purpose and vision may sometimes seem to be inhibited by your circumstances. There will likely be times when it looks as if your gifts or purpose doesn't fit the setting. Or there may be days when others look down on the specific gifts God has given you to be who he has called you to be. And there will be days when it may

And we know that in all things God works for the good of those who love him, who have been called according to his purpose. **Romans 8:28**

seem you are fighting flesh and blood, but it is really the powers and principalities of the darkness. This is the reality of living in a fallen world, waiting for heaven to come.

Yet no matter what, you can endure and persist even when circumstances or people seem to oppose your vision. In fact, it is very likely that in the most trying times your values will be tested and refined, to become the roots on which are grown the behaviors you will need to adhere to when living out your purpose and vision in the present and future.

I pray that the tools from this lesson will help you articulate your purpose, vision, and values in concrete and tangible ways.

Why?

So that you can return again and again to an artifact that reminds you of who you were created to be and the specific assignments that you are gifted to complete "for the common good" (the unified work of God's people) (1 Corinthians 12:7). I pray that you will *Go & See* a new or greater picture of how to live in step with your God-given design, no matter what. Most of all, I pray that you will *see* yourself as God *sees* you and that, from that point of view, you will operate with power, delight, and wholeness.

 ## Reflection & Application

To help with clarity, here are brief definitions for *purpose*, *vision*, and *values*:

- **Purpose**: The reasons I am set in my place and time.
- **Vision**: The specific accomplishments that will happen through me.
- **Values**: Behaviors I will need to commit to in order to live out my purpose and vision.

In this lesson, the book of Hebrews and the story of Joseph's life are going to help us *see* that staying steady in purpose and committed to vision requires living by values and in close relationship to the Holy Spirit—the one able to sustain our faith. In addition, you will *see* through these Bible passages that remaining faithful to using the gifts and vision entrusted to you right where you are brings glory to God and fulfillment of purpose and vision.

Steadiness is built on faith, truth, and trust: **Faith** in a God whom you cannot see, but whom you can know. **Truth** that comes from God's word, the Holy Spirit, and revelation. **Trust** that your God has a good plan for you, even when your location and vocation don't quite match what you imagined them to be.

Let's first *Go & See* how faith, truth, and trust enable us to fulfill our God-given destinies. *Go* and read Hebrews, chapters 11–13, and highlight the verses that point to how one lives out his or her God-given purpose and vision.

Now take a few minutes to reflect on Hebrews 11–13 and the applications it has for our lives. Pull out your journal and get to a quiet place of mind. Then answer each question as fully as possible. Check off each one as you *go*.

- ❏ **1)** What do you interpret (*infer/conclude*) from the repetition of the phrase *by faith* in Hebrews, chapter 11?
  - ❏ What part does it look as though faith plays in vision?
- ❏ **2)** What does Hebrews 12:1–3 show us Jesus's vision was?
  - ❏ How did this vision help him complete his mission?
- ❏ **3)** Do you believe God has a specific "race marked out" for you?
  - ❏ How could believing this help you in living more boldly into your purpose and vision?
- ❏ **4)** What does Hebrews 13 say about the "values" of those who live, purposefully in line with God's vision for them?
  - ❏ **a)** List the specific behaviors that are mentioned as acceptable.
  - ❏ **b)** List the specific behaviors that are mentioned as unacceptable.
- ❏ **5)** Why do you think "values" (behaviors) are necessary to successfully living out your purpose and vision?

We have all been given talents that we are asked to invest [multiply] until the day our master returns and asks us to give an account for what we did with what he gave us.
Matthew 25:14-30

Notes:

Digging Deeper

As you have now reflected on Hebrews, are you beginning to *see* that faith is the first step toward living out the purpose and vision God has set in you? By **faith** we move in the direction of his purpose via the design he has knit into us. By **faith** we step into the plans he has for us to use our gifts to accomplish visions. Hebrews 12 reveals that ***fixing our eyes on Jesus*** is how we run our race. Jesus fixed his eyes on the joy of saving us from our sins at the cross. The vision of the outcome helped him to endure the cross because he saw the need to get to the other side of death on the cross—our redemption!

Lastly, Hebrews 13 defines for us the values (*behaviors*) that will help us move steadily forward in our purposes. But let's dig even deeper into the story of a man who shows us what it looks like to remain steady in purpose, vision, and values, even in unexpected and undesirable circumstances. Values prevail when purpose and vision seem nowhere in sight.

Take a few minutes to *Go & See* the details of the story of Joseph recorded in Genesis 37:1–11 and Genesis 50:15–21. Highlight the verses that stick out to you. Then come back.

Did you *see* the following?

- Joseph's brothers hated his dreams (*a gift from God*) and his coat (*a gift from his father*). He had favor from his father and favor from God. This made them jealous. Joseph's flaunting it maybe didn't help. But remember, he was very young at this time.
- There is a purpose in suffering—it can mature us.
- Joseph didn't earn his favor, either from his father or from God.
- The number of years between Joseph's dreams and the fulfillment of them was likely three decades.
- Be prepared to let God use your gifts and fulfill your visions and dreams in his timing.
- God will not let you step into living your purpose and vision before you are ready. He will prepare you. This is for your good and the goodness of his purposes through you.

Joseph's Story Reveals Purpose, Vision, and Values: Joseph, who is considered a prototype or prefigure of Christ, says in looking back on his 30 years of persisting in his purpose while being a slave, "God intended it all for good to accomplish what is now being done, the saving of many lives" (Genesis 50:20).

We see in Joseph persistence, consistency, and discipline in operating out of his giftings in all his circumstances. It is plausible to conclude: Joseph was persistent in honoring God with his life because his trust in the purpose and vision God had given him was greater than the suffering found in his circumstances. He was consistent in devoting all that he did to God because he believed in the dreams and visions that were given to him. And he was disciplined in making decisions based on his values (*not* on his circumstances or emotions, *nor* to please others), which likely altered his attitude and perspective on his circumstances.

How was he able to stay true to who God had made him to be despite the fact that he was in horrible circumstances due to jealousy and false accusations (*and maybe a little bit because of his own haughtiness*)?

He had a vision (literal dreams), given to him from God, and he chose to live toward it even when it seemed the vision had died with the animal's blood that was shed to drench his coat of many colors—and were deferred again after he was sold into slavery. And again after he was unjustly put in prison.

We too can ask God to give us a picture, vision, or dream of what he has planned for us. We too should maybe plan for the possibility that it might take a few years or decades to come to fruition. We too can persist even when it seems we aren't where we planned to be, because we can trust the outcome of living for God to be in line with his goodness.

You can use all the tools from this study, along with asking for revelation and discernment from the Holy Spirit, to write out a purpose statement, a vision statement, and a set of values that can guide you no matter what circumstances you find yourself in. With these as guides, you can also have a clearer picture of God's delight in you, enabling you to:

- have **FAITH** in a God whom we cannot see but whom we can know;
- live by the **TRUTH** that comes from God's word, the Holy Spirit, and revelation; and
- **TRUST** that our God has a good plan for us, even when our location or vocation doesn't quite match the environments we imagined God would lead us to, based on our gifts and visions.

 ## Tool 8: Purpose, Vision and Values Statements

Purpose, Vision, and Values Statements: A document recording who you are, where you are going, and how you will get there.

This tool helps you document a purpose, vision, and values statement for yourself or your family. This can be powerful in claiming persistence, consistency, and discipline over the gifts, purpose, and vision God has given you.

It isn't the tool that makes you able and powerful; rather, the power comes from the Holy Spirit's presence in you as you work. However, these tools can help tether you to remembrance and guide you in decision making in times of high emotions, confusion, or transition. Also, these tools can be like a mirror for you to return to and again rightly *see* who God has made you to be and what he intends for you to accomplish when you get a little bit lost.

The definitions* of these words—purpose, vision, and values—and the questions included within each will be what you use to create statements that both reflect what you were designed to accomplish and provide a guidepost for you to return to again and again— especially when it comes time to say *yes* to this or *no* to that.

Purpose Defined

Just as Jesus was sent down to earth with a purpose set under the will of God, so too are we. John 6:38 says, "I have come down to heaven not to do my will but to do the will of he who sent me." We are to look upward to grasp our purpose for our days here on this earth. It is written out in heaven; our job is to unpack it and to live it out well right where we are now—and then also to submit the outcome to the goodness we know of God's greater plans for our lives.

You have done a lot of unpacking over the course of the last seven lessons. So you have all you need to start articulating your purpose. Don't forget what you've discovered through your personal history, assessing your unique design, and *seeing* the impact of relationships on your life. Remember to remember. You may need to *go* back to these to *see* forward.

Don't worry if your purpose statement is not specific or detailed at first; you can write it out and begin living it out even while it is still being revised and edited. As you seek the Lord for more understanding, you can always return and revise, adding in details that bring clarity. As seasons of life change, the essence of your purpose statement will remain, but the "for whom" or the "outcome" may change. So don't get stuck on making the wording perfect or expect to arrive at a statement that could encompass all of your life from now until the end.

Vision Defined

Vision is a dream with a direction and is based on your natural talents, spiritual gifts, personality traits, and personal history. The Holy Spirit's promptings and power provide you with understanding and clarity. In other words, vision is a landscape picture of a future you intend to create (*work toward/bring to fruition*) by using the gifts and unique design you've been given. Painting vision requires you to *Go & See* (*uncover*) what you have and imagine how it will look when you invest what you've been given. Paramount to aligning the outcome of your vision to God's restoration plan is focusing on *seeing* how your vision will support the "common good" (1 Corinthians 12:7) of the church, your family, or society.

You have already gone and uncovered your gifts with the tools of the last seven lessons. Your reflections, artifacts, and charts completed using the tools from each lesson, along with the abiding presence of the Holy Spirit, are all you need to boldly and excitedly put words down to claim and document the vision you *see* set in you by our creator. He delights in your discovery of the visions he has set in you. He can't wait for you to write them down.

Values Defined

Values are behaviors you will choose to live out, no matter what, because you believe they are in line with the purpose and vision given to you by your creator. These need defining and describing in order to be effective. In addition, rooting each in scripture breathes life into them and tethers them to truth.

Joseph lived his values regardless of his circumstances. He never quit using his gifts of interpreting dreams, leadership, or truth-telling. Even in prison. Let this encourage you to do the same. Or think of it this way: if I want to run a marathon well, then I need to commit to running a certain amount of miles based on a plan that slowly increases mileage from week to week. But I also need to make changes to what I eat and how much I sleep. The vision to run a marathon changes more decisions about my life than just adding running to my day. It requires me to commit to a set of values, displayed through behaviors and disciplines. So too with committing to live out a vision of any other kind.

Defining your values can be incredibly helpful in decision making and determining how to take action in ways that align with your values (*versus acting based on circumstances, emotions, or pleasing others*). Eventually, when this tool is used to help you stay committed to and focused on living out your values daily, you will likely see changes in how you live and clarity in purpose and vision coming to fruition. Also, remember that even when it looks as if your vision and dreams are not working out, you will be growing in character and strength—just like Joseph—by staying committed to living out your values regardless of your circumstances.

 ## Instructions

As you brainstorm ideas and put words to thoughts, do not let circumstances, fear, or comparison hinder what you write. Answer each question authentically and boldly. Try to make the answers personal and specific to your design, rather than general or intangible statements that encompass the Christian life. Remember to look back to *see* forward.

❑   Day 1: **Write Your Purpose Statement**: After examining the results of the tools you used to take inventory of your giftings and personality, along with your personal history and ***Relationship Investment Plan***, use the following to begin to define your purpose statement:

❑   Purpose Prewriting Question

- ❑ Day 2: **Write Your Vision Statement**: After examining the results of the tools you used to take inventory of your giftings and personality, along with your personal history and **Relationship Investment Plan**, use the following to define your vision statement:
- ❑ Vision Prewriting Questions
- ❑ Days 3–4: **Define Your Values** (*Definitions + Behaviors*): Based on the results of the tools you used so far in this study, consider what values will be necessary in order for you to live toward your purpose and vision, and to develop in your areas of giftings. Use the following to determine and define your values:
- ❑ Values and Behaviors Idea Generator
- ❑ Defining Values Prewriting Questions
- ❑ Defining Values Grid
- ❑ Day 5: **Purpose, Vision, and Values Summary**: This is the final action step of this study! Using the instructions given in *The Next Step* portion of this lesson, look back on all your prewriting activities related to purpose, vision, and values. There are two different ways for you to complete the summary. Choose the **one** that works best for you:
- ❑ Free-write into paragraphs or bullet points onto the blank page provided.
- ❑ Use the "My Purpose, Vision & Values Summary."

The Next Step

Now, it is time to write or type your purpose, vision, and values into a single document (*space provided on the last page of this lesson*). And make a plan to share what you have written with a close friend or spouse.

In the writing process there are five steps: (1) **Prewriting**: brainstorming, researching, outlining; (2) **Drafting**: getting ideas onto paper; (3) **Revising**: adjusting organization and expanding on details to make ideas clearer; (4) **Editing**: improving grammar, mechanics, and formatting; (5) **Publishing**: making the text ready to be viewed by others.

The entire journey from start to finish can take some authors multiple years to complete. As you write out your purpose, vision, and values, expect to be somewhat dissatisfied with the words, ideas, organization, or overall writing style at first. Yet you also need to know that it is much easier to revise words that are imperfect than it is to retrieve perfect words in drafting-mode. Embrace the process.

So get a draft down by completing all the prewriting steps, and then *go* back to revise later. *Going* back will likely be a struggle. Without an audience or deadlines, getting to step five of the writing process will require self-motivation, grit, and a plan. The best way I have found to accomplish this feat is to find my own audience. Meaning, I invite someone to read or listen to my words and give me feedback. Your audience can be anyone in your life—a friend, a family member, your spouse, a mentor, a small group, a pastor, or a co-worker. Setting them up as your audience is actually pretty simple.

First, contact the person or people you are comfortable sharing your purpose, vision, and values with. Let them know you've been working on something you would like to share and that you would really value their listening ear. Then set up a day and time (*give yourself at least two weeks to revise and edit*) to either meet in person or to email your document to your "audience."

Ta-da! You've given yourself a deadline and an audience and increased the likelihood that you will move from having a draft to having a document that has been revised, edited, and published for the audience you have coming to meet you.

On a spiritual level, taking this next step of finding an audience invites another person to know your purpose, vision, and values—providing accountability, support, and quite possibly increased Holy Spirit power. God *sees* us working on articulating the purpose, vision, and values he has set in each of us, but too often we don't let others in to *see*. And we don't often feel His eyes are on us until a brother or sister sits with us and affirms us with encouraging words or nods of agreement.

Jesus said in Matthew 18:20, "Where two or three gather in my name, there am I with them." Inviting an audience of one or more to read or listen to what you have written is an invitation to your soul and theirs to gather in Jesus's name and experience his presence. It gives you a deadline and at the same time creates a space for someone to ask you clarifying questions, affirm you, and pray over you to live out your purpose, vision, and values no matter your present circumstances or season of life.

Post your document in a place where you will be reminded to daily, weekly, or monthly read, pray, and act on what has been revealed to you.

Closing

Your gifts point you toward your purpose, vision, and values. Have you fully discovered and unwrapped your gifts yet?

If not, what is holding you back?

Stop and pray for strength to fight the good fight of faith to uncover all the ways you have been designed to live out your purpose and vision. Draw momentum to propel you forward in your journey from the fact that God delights in you discovering all the ways he made you

God desires for us to *Go & See* how what we have can meet the needs of the "multitudes" when he miraculously multiplies the little bit we have.
Mark 6:30-44

to meet the needs around you. Ultimately, put loving him deeply and finding joy in his destiny for you at the center of why you keep seeking understanding of yourself and him.

Throughout the process of articulating (*in writing*) your purpose, vision, and values, remember that you are on a journey to discover what was established before the beginning of time; your work is to excavate, seek to understand, increase, and enjoy. As you use words to hone in on clarity, also keep in mind that your circumstances don't determine your giftings, your purpose, your vision, or your ability to live committed to your values. Proximity to God does. Who you are where you are is more significant than where you are and the circumstances around you.

To circle back to Lesson 1, your purpose statement, vision statement, and list of values can be like stones of remembrance (Joshua 4), allowing you to remain steadily pointed in the direction God has your heart created to run. It is worth your time and energy to keep a record of the purpose, vision, and values etched into your soul. We are forgetful; that makes us human. This document can help you always remember never to forget.

In addition, the process of articulating purpose, vision, and values helps you *Go & See* all that God has done to reveal himself to you, design you, and purpose you to "greater things" (John 14:12–14). All through Christ who gives you strength (Philippians 4:13). Your investment in the "talents" given to you is not optional because God's plans for bringing glory to his name and redemption to his people include you.

In the end, the ultimate purpose in working with the tools from this lesson is for you to grasp the ways that Mark 6:30–44 is to be applied to your life.

What do you have?

Go & See.

Now, how will you use what you have found to "feed" the multitude in front of you?

You were made to run your race right now. In Christ, you have everything you need to live on purpose, for his purposes, to fulfill your redeemed heart's visions, for the glory of God and the love of the people he has placed in your spaces. Believe this. Live this. Bring others with you. Watch and *see* what miracles God does along the way.

The definitions and process provided for articulating purpose, vision and values in the Go & See study have been adapted with permission from the Servant Leadership RoundTable course, from Triune Leadership Services.

Purpose Prewriting Questions

Purpose: The reasons I am set in my place and time.

A **Purpose Statement** answers the question, *Why did God set me in this generation (time) and this place (location and vocation)?* Other questions that can help you articulate a complete answer to this question:

- ❑ What past experiences have shaped what I enjoy doing?
- ❑ What are my spiritual gifts?
- ❑ What are my natural talents?
- ❑ How do I best (based on personality type) process and interact with the world around me?
- ❑ What relationships/experiences have matured me?
- ❑ Who (what person or type of people) do I get most excited to serve?
- ❑ What do I desire to do/create/invest in?
- ❑ What is the intended outcome or value of doing/creating/investing in it?

Answer the following questions incorporating the words, phrases, and ideas from your inventories and reflections.

1. What gifts and resources did I *see* I have based on the Go & See tools? (List all your gifts and resources.)

2. What do I hope (dream) to do with the gifts (listed above) I have been given?

3. Who will benefit from me accomplishing this dream?

4. Why is what I hope to accomplish important (to me and for others)?

5. Then narrow down your answers to create a purpose statement that might look something like this:

I, _____ (name) am created and gifted with the following gifts, _____ to provide
_____.
to or for _____.
so they can _____
_____.

Vision Prewriting Questions

Vision: The specific accomplishments, changes, impact or outcome that will happen through me (when I am using my gifts to accomplish my purpose).

A **Vision Statement** answers the question, *What did God design me to do/create/become because of who I am and what I have been given?* Other questions that can help you articulate a complete answer to this question:

- ❑ What do the themes from my personal history reveal to me about my future vision?
- ❑ What spiritual gifts will be used in me to accomplish this vision?
- ❑ What natural talents have I been given to accomplish my vision?
- ❑ Who has invested in me? How can I invest in a similar way in others?
- ❑ What can I give to those around me for such a time as this?
- ❑ What pressing desire has God set on my heart?

Based on the results of the tools you used to take inventory of your giftings, design, and purpose, answer the following questions incorporating the words, phrases, and ideas from your inventories and reflections. The goal is to *Go & See* a vision of your future. (You can determine how far away that future is.)

1. What do you desire most to accomplish/do/create/build/invest in? (*In five years, ten years, … by the end of my life.*)

2. How will society or the body of Christ benefit as a result of you pursuing your vision (what you desire to accomplish)?

3. What will you need (e.g., materials, people, training, education) in order to successfully impact others for Christ through accomplishing your vision?

4. What would God say about the vision you intend to fulfill? (Why will he delight in you working toward and accomplishing your vision?)

5. Synthesize your answers from above to create a description of the vision (preferred future) you see for yourself or your family. (For help with ideas, see examples in the appendix.)

Values and Behaviors Idea Generator

Using the descriptions of the values below found in 1 Corinthians 13:4–7 and Galatians 5:22–23, fill in the chart to help you generate ideas for the values and behaviors you will need in order to live out your purpose and vision statements.

Value & Passage	Definition of Value	Behaviors that demonstrate living out the value	Examples of behaviors (actions)
Love			Helping others with a task Spending time with someone Listening to someone's problems
Patience			Waiting w/o becoming angry Not interrupting people
Joy			Smile more Be happy for those who accomplish something I didn't

Value & Passage	Definition of Value	Behaviors that demonstrate living out the value	Examples of behaviors (actions)
Peace			Calm attitude during stressful times Praying for self and others to have peace
Kindness			Doing the dishes or laundry without being asked Saying hello, making eye contact Hug or high-five (or elbow bump)
Self-control			Not eating a whole pan of brownies Holding my tongue Prayer/ quiet time
Faithfulness			Prayer Forgiveness (loyalty) Following through with promises and commitments

Defining Values Prewriting Questions

Values: Behaviors I will need to commit to in order to live my purpose and vision.

A **Values Statement** answers the question, *How am I going to behave in order to be diligent in working toward my purpose and vision?* Other questions that can help you articulate a complete answer to this question:

- ❑ What kind of character-traits do I need to develop in order to live toward my purpose and vision?
- ❑ What habits or disciplines will I commit to in order to allow space for my gifts to develop and mature?
- ❑ What "fruits of the Spirit" will I pursue with intentionality, so that God can use me no matter where I am?

Answer the following questions, incorporating the words, phrases, and ideas from your inventories and reflections.

1. What *values* and *behaviors* will you need to *commit to* in order to focus on living in alignment with the gifts, purpose, and vision God has given to you (for this season or beyond)? *List as many as you can think of.*

2. Then circle or highlight 3–5 values you want to focus on intentionally growing. Base your list of values on any of the following: your gifts, inventory activities, the Values and Behaviors Idea Generator, your purpose, and vision statements.

Defining Your Values Grid

What *values* and *behaviors* will you need to *commit to* in order to focus on living in alignment with the gifts, purpose, and vision God has given to you (for this season or beyond)?

This grid can help you clarify and measure each value's definition and behaviors that will demonstrate you are living out that value. Try to thoroughly work through at least three, and no more than five. These form the beginning of living a life of purpose on purpose. To be useful, values need to be defined in terms of specific behaviors.

Value	Definition	Behaviors	Scripture Support

Value	Definition	Behaviors	Scripture Support

Value	Definition	Behaviors	Scripture Support

Value	Definition	Behaviors	Scripture Support

My Purpose, Vision & Values Summary

Use the space below to write your purpose, vision, and values into a single document. Share what you have written with a close friend, parent, mentor, pastor, youth leader, or spouse. Post your document in a place where you will be reminded often to read, pray over, and act on what has been revealed to you.

My purpose is to use my resources & gifts of ...
(list spiritual gifts, natural talents, and resources in the boxes)

My Resources (training, knowledge, materials gained from personal experiences)	**My Gifts** (spiritual gifts, natural talents, & personality strengths)

To do/create/invest in or for (to do what or for whom) ...

_____

_____

So they can ...

_____

_____

My Vision Statement

Take your answers from **Purpose Prewriting** and **Writing Your Vision Statement** and formulate them into a vision paragraph below.

_____

_____

_____

_____

_____

_____

_____

_____

_____

_____

_____

The Values I Am Committed To

Value	Behavior	Scripture Support

Sendoff

Purpose and Context

God desires for us to Go & See how what we have can meet the needs of the "multitudes" when he miraculously multiplies the little bit we have.

Mark 6:30-44

We have all been given talents that we are asked to invest [multiply] until the day our master returns and asks us to give an account for what we did with what he gave us.

Matthew 25:14-30

We are forgetful. Thus, we need to set-up "stones of remembrance" as markers of God's faithfulness, strength and involvement in our journey.

Joshua 4

Send-Off

We love God well by loving others extraordinarily. This is our purpose. This is our calling. This is what we were made for. American culture will tell us to pursue comfort, control, and self-improvement. But let's be the ones who choose to believe and live out the belief that we were designed on purpose, given gifts to fulfill that purpose, and provided power to accomplish that purpose through Christ who gives us strength (Philippians 4:13).

We *don't feel* this purpose. We *live* this purpose with action and intentionality. We *don't guess* at what this purpose is. We *know* this purpose because of the words of the Bible, the instructions of the Holy Spirit, and the encouragement of the body of Christ.

Overall entities of his creation, God spoke into each one its name and its purpose. Before an expanse, creature, or human being was formed, first God's words spoke to what it would be and the purpose it would have. Out of the truth of his words, each came to life to live as intended by the creator.

Chew on that thought for a bit. Let it sink into your mind and soul.

If God spoke into existence all that we see, and if his naming and purpose for each were set in place by his words at the beginning of time, then purpose and gifts were set into each of us at the beginning of time with his words.

Friends, our purpose isn't out there waiting for us to create or mold. Our purpose isn't a mystery we wait on the right words to come up with to define. Nope. Your purpose is not dependent on what you do or what you see. Rather, it is set in you. It may need some unwrapping. You will likely need to work at understanding it and walking in it. But it isn't going anywhere. And it isn't up to you to create it.

Why?

Because what God speaks never returns void (Isaiah 55:11). What he placed into motion at creation is still true; it just sometimes gets a little tainted by the sin that entered the world. But we have the power to fight back the lies and the false perceptions (Isaiah 54:17). Plus, we have the Spirit who gives us the ability to believe that the words of scripture are true of us (John 7:38).

Let's not be of those who shrink back (Hebrews 10:39), but those who by faith overcome through the blood of the lamb and the word of our testimony (Revelation 12:11). And let's not keep that testimony to ourselves because we just might have the story that another needs to hear to be set free.

You are of the "chosen people, a royal priesthood, a holy nation, God's special possession, that you may declare the praises of him who called you out of darkness into his wonderful light" (1 Peter 2:9). And who knows if you haven't been set in this time and place in order that many lives may be saved because of your obedience in fulfilling all that he has called you to for such a time as this (Esther 4:14)?

Relentlessly cry out for wisdom, and beg for understanding; seek both, and you will know God (Proverbs 2:3–5). And he will gently, slowly, and faithfully help you excavate the talents he has given you to invest now and until the day he returns and asks for an account of all that you have done with what he has given you (Matthew 25:14–30). Believe and obey, and by grace and faith one day you will hear from the savior of your life, "Well done, my good and faithful servant. Come and enter my kingdom forever."

In the end, no other words will matter—only this: Love God. Love others. Make disciples. You have all that is necessary to do so. This may be hard to feel or *see* from time to time. In those times, get away on the other side of the lake with Jesus and his disciples, and *Go & See* what you have already been given to obey God and meet the needs of those around you. His miracles of multiplication, nourishment, and rest are right on the other side of your obedience. Understanding, joy, and strength await you there. Return often. He will always be there, ready to provide exactly what you need because he delights in watching you do greater things than you can ask for or imagine (Ephesians 3:20). He has made you for purposes that he has already destined you to fulfill. *Go & See*.

Then *go* and inspire and equip others to do the same.

Notes:

Small Group Guide

Tips & Lesson by Lesson Instruction

Small Group Study Guide Expectations

If you are using this study in a small group, what follows is a guide to help you process and reflect during your times of meeting together. As I mentioned at the start, there are not weeks or days listed within the book because I recognize and want to honor that we all work, learn, reflect, and process at a different pace. However, I also believe very strongly in the power of gathering together on a journey, because when we travel together, we hold one another accountable, encourage each other to keep going, and provide prayer covering that has more power than we even comprehend.

So know that this study is an excellent resource for a small group to tackle together. But also be prepared to allow deadlines to be somewhat loose and to be overly encouraging of the group members to show up, even if they didn't complete the predetermined lesson for the group meeting day.

That said, it is helpful to set some expectations for your group meeting time. Below are some that I would encourage you to set and lead with during your times together.

1. **Pursue Deep Conversations** – It can be hard to jump right into below-the-surface conversations; however, it is worth your time and discomfort to do so. With grace and gentleness, guide small group discussions to remain focused on the content of the study, sharing personal revelations gained from working through the lesson, and tying thoughts and ideas back to the truth and promises of the Bible.
2. **Commit to Being Consistent and Present** – Again, *consistent* is not the same as *completed*. Challenge the members of your group to work at a pace that is consistent and works for them, and to show up even if they didn't get through an entire lesson. And then commit to being fully present during the meeting time, not distracted by phones or other devices that fit in one's purse or pocket. Set a tone of simplicity and structure so that members of the group feel comfortable and invited.
3. **Be Considerate of Others' Stories and Reflections** – Share answers concisely, so that all are able to contribute to the discussion. This doesn't mean stay shallow; instead, go

deep from the start. Also, keep the stories others share confidential. It is brave and bold to share our lives with others, building a culture of trust by not allowing anything shared in the group to leave the group. Lastly, this study is about processing and leaning into the voice of God for direction and asking for insight from the Holy Spirit for understanding. And the purpose of the group meetings is to direct one another to God and the Holy Spirit as each one processes, reflects, and records. To that end, encourage everyone to avoid counseling. Rather, choose affirmation, encouragement, and scripture to spur one another on.

Small Group Study Guide Leader's General Instructions

Thank you for choosing to use your gifts to lead a small group through *Go & See*. I hope both you and those who are attending are blessed by your leadership. I pray you will experience joy and peace in new and deeper ways because of the role you play in the lives of the women who experience this study with you as their guide.

Below is a suggested outline of how to progress through the study with your small group. Know, however, that as you take into the process all that is happening with your group, it's reasonable to adjust the "plan." Trust your insight, and ask the Holy Spirit for specific instructions when you are sensing that your group may need to detour from the suggestions at times.

Basic Outline for Each Group Session:

1. **Meet and Greet**. Connect with one another on the most basic things that make up your life—jobs, kids, husbands, pets, etc.
2. **Pray**. This is crucial. Invite the Holy Spirit to be present. Allow for silence as you wait upon his presence to be felt and revealed. On the first night I would challenge you to take turns laying hands on one another, praying over each that she would experience the power, insight, and understanding needed to draw near to the Lord's heart on this journey.
3. **Discuss the Reflection & Application Questions**. Each lesson includes a set of questions at the end of the Reflection & Application section. These will be your starting point each week.
4. **Share Progress Made with the Tool of the Lesson**. Each lesson has a tool—a set of instructions to complete an assignment designed to help each person *Go & See* her unique design. Each person shares the progress she has made and any insights she has gleaned.
5. **Read the Closing**. Read aloud the "Closing" section of the lesson. Dismiss.

Tips for Leading:

1. **Pray & Trust:** Set aside time throughout the week to pray for the women walking through the study with you. Trust that God is doing the transformational work, and he is smiling down on you for giving of your time and resources to allow women the opportunity to experience *Go & See* together. The outcomes of the study aren't up to you or me. We are

both trusting God to use our "two fish and five loaves" to do miracles that are beyond our comprehension.

2. **Guide & Coach**: Don't be afraid to ask the hard questions that could help someone move out of inconsistencies and into consistency. When you see women showing up without any work completed, be quick to let them know their presence is a blessing to you. But also, ask them what's up—why isn't the work being done? And then ask them if you can do anything that would help keep them consistent in progressing in the study.

3. **Be about Relationships**: Encourage all members of the group to exchange phone numbers and emails so that they can be in touch with one another in between sessions. You can't possibly connect deeply with each person attending, so build a norm within the group that propels them to connect to one another. You can also use other social media forms to be connected. Use those to the degree they are helpful and not overwhelming or adding stress to your life.

Tips for Organizing:

1. **Invite:** Personally invite a few women to join you for this study, or ask your pastor if you can invite women from the church. Either way, if your group is bigger than six, when it comes to discussion time, try to break up into groups of three or four. This allows each person more time to share and may allow some to feel more comfortable sharing because of the smaller number of ears listening.

2. **Secure a Location & Dates:** After securing a location, set the meeting times in advance, and barring emergencies, don't change the dates. If it is a bigger group, find a location where it is easy for small groups to break away so that those who have a hard time hearing in big crowds are able to hear the people sharing in their small group. **Plan for each meeting session to go two hours**.

3. **Order Books**: Once you know about how many people will be joining you for the study, order the books. If you haven't experienced the study yourself, try to be one lesson ahead of the group so that at the end of each meeting you can give them a heads-up on any materials they might need for the coming lesson. (For example, Lesson 2 requires highlighters, and Lesson 3 requires some rocks and sharpies. You don't need to provide these, as most people have them at home. But letting them know about the materials needed will help them prepare for the coming lesson.)

4. **Plan and Prepare**. Plan to collect phone numbers and emails on the first evening so that you can help women stay connected. Also, since they won't have their books prior to the first gathering, your first meeting will not look like the other meetings. Prepare to have women introduce one another, read through all introductory pages together, and go over the Small Group Study Guide Expectations.

Small Group Study Guide
Lesson by Lesson Instructions

Meeting Session 1: Use the first gathering session to build connections and establish norms and culture for your group. At this session members will also become familiar with the structure and goals of the study.

1. Welcome women, and have them share what brought them to attend this study, and any other icebreaker questions you choose to come up with.
2. Hand out copies of the book, and help everyone become familiar with the instructions and expectations of the study by doing the following:
   2.1 Read aloud the "Dear Reader" letter.
   2.2 Read aloud the Small Group Study Guide Expectations
   2.3 Have members (on their own) page through the Small Group Study Guide Lesson by Lesson Instructions to be aware of what is ahead.
   2.4 Ask for questions or clarifications on location, times, or dates and expectations.
3. Split into pairs to do the following:
   3.1 With a partner read the "About This Study" section.
   3.2 Share with the same partner your hopes and prayers in doing this study.
   3.3 Each person then takes turns laying hands on and praying over their partner.
4. Return to the large group and read aloud, "What do you have? Go and See." And ask the group to confirm that each person is ready to accept the invitation of the study and make consistent progress throughout your journey together.
5. Guide the group through flipping through sections of Lesson 1, reminding them of what was written in the "About This Study" section. Encourage them to determine the days and times they will work on the study in advance, so that they can come prepared to the next meeting.
6. Close with reminding attendees of the next meeting date and a prayer.
7. Dismiss.

Meeting Session 2: Sessions 2–8 will follow the same general outline. If there are changes to the usual outline, they will be listed as bold for the session.

1. **Meet and Greet**. Connect with one another on the most basic things that make up your life—jobs, kids, husbands, pets, etc.
2. **Pray**. This is crucial. Invite the Holy Spirit to be present. Allow for silence as you wait upon his presence to be felt and revealed.
3. **Discuss the Reflection & Application Questions**. Each lesson includes a set of questions at the end of the Reflection & Application section. These will be your starting point each week. (If the group is larger than six people, split into small groups at this time.) **At this meeting, discuss Lesson 1, Reflection & Application questions.**
4. **Share Progress Made with the Tool of the Lesson**. Each lesson has a tool—a set of instructions to complete an assignment designed to help each person *Go & See* her unique design. Each person shares the progress she has made and any insights she has gleaned. **At this meeting, share your Stones of Remembrance Timeline, and what you learned while putting it together.**
5. **Read the Closing**. Briefly overview Lesson 2, and let the group know they'll need highlighters to complete the Tool section. **Read aloud "Closing" of Lesson 1**.
6. Dismiss.

Meeting Session 3: The discussion and content for Lesson 2 is much less than Lesson 1. So plan on giving the group 30–45 minutes of work time during this meeting session to either catch up or move forward. If people have not yet done "The Next Step" section of Lesson 1 or Lesson 2, direct them to do so during work time. A few times throughout the study there is work time built in during the meeting sessions because sometimes what holds us back from processing is quiet space to do so. Don't overtake the work time with more discussion. Many people will need this time to process.

1. **Meet and Greet**. Connect with one another on the most basic things that make up your life—jobs, kids, husbands, pets, etc.
2. **Pray**. This is crucial. Invite the Holy Spirit to be present. Allow for silence as you wait upon his presence to be felt and revealed.
3. **Discuss the Reflection & Application Questions**. Each lesson includes a set of questions at the end of the Reflection & Application section. These will be your starting point each week. (If the group is larger than six people, split into small groups at this time.) **At this meeting, discuss Lesson 2, Reflection & Application questions.**
4. **Share Progress Made with the Tool of the Lesson**. Each lesson has a tool—a set of instructions to complete an assignment designed to help each person *Go & See* her unique design. Each person shares the progress she has made and any insights she has gleaned. **At this meeting, share your Thematic Labeling of Stones, and what you learned while putting it together.**

5. **Individual Processing and Reflection Time: Allow 30–45 minutes of work time during this meeting session to either catch up or move forward.** (See meeting session 3 instructions for more details.)

6. **Read the Closing**. Briefly overview Lesson 3, and let the group know they'll need a few rocks, a sharpie, and a place of solitude to complete the Tool section of Lesson 3. Also, let them know Lesson 3 is very experiential and may feel a bit out of the norm, but encourage them to embrace the activity and trust that God will use it to bring insight and freedom. **Read aloud "Closing" of Lesson 2.**

7. Dismiss.

Meeting Session 4: The discussion and content for Lesson 3 is less than Lesson 1. And what is required from Lesson 4 is going to be more time-consuming than any previous lesson. So still plan on giving the group 30 minutes of work time during this meeting session to either catch up or move forward. **But also plan on using more time for the closing to go over the Tool 4: Writing a Personal Essay Instructions.** If people have not yet done "The Next Step" section for Lesson 1, Lesson 2, or Lesson 3, direct them to do so during work time. Or they can begin working on Lesson 4.

1. **Meet and Greet**. Connect with one another on the most basic things that make up your life—jobs, kids, husbands, pets, etc.

2. **Pray**. This is crucial. Invite the Holy Spirit to be present. Allow for silence as you wait upon his presence to be felt and revealed.

3. **Discuss the Reflection & Application Questions**. Each lesson includes a set of questions at the end of the Reflection & Application section. These will be your starting point each week. (If the group is larger than six people, split into small groups at this time.) **At this meeting, discuss Lesson 3, Reflection & Application questions.**

4. **Share Progress Made with the Tool of the Lesson**. Each lesson has a tool—a set of instructions to complete an assignment designed to help each person *Go & See* her unique design. Each person shares the progress she has made and any insights she has gleaned. **At this meeting, share your Stone Washing Activity Reflection, and what you learned while putting it together.**

5. **Individual Processing and Reflection Time: Allow 30 minutes of work time during this meeting session to either catch up or move forward.** (See meeting session 3 instructions, above, for more details.)

6. **Read the Closing**. Briefly overview Lesson 4. **Together, read through the Personal Essay Writing Instructions** and note that Tool 4: Writing a Personal Essay, may take six days to complete. So this lesson will likely be more time-consuming than any of the previous lessons. And having access to one's timeline from Lesson 1 and thematic labeling from Lesson 2 will be necessary. **Read aloud "Closing" of Lesson 3.**

7. Dismiss.

Meeting Session 5: This session is structured differently in order to allow the maximum amount of time for people to share their personal essays with the group.

1. **Meet and Greet.** Connect with one another on the most basic things that make up your life—jobs, kids, husbands, pets, etc.

2. **Pray.** This is crucial. Invite the Holy Spirit to be present. Allow for silence as you wait upon his presence to be felt and revealed.

3. **Gather Your Thoughts.** Allow a few minutes for people to review their essays and mentally and emotionally prepare to share them.

4. **Partner Sharing Time.** Find a partner, and each share your essay. (No commentary, just read what is written).

5. **Group Sharing Time.** After nerves have been worked out in the partner sharing, gather everyone together. If your group is larger than fifteen people, split into two small groups for this. If not, remain together as a larger group. Allow time for everyone to share their Personal Essay. Not everyone has to share, but make sure not to stop this early. Long silences are okay. Some people need them to muster up the courage to share.

6. **Read the Closing.** Briefly overview Lesson 5. **Together, read through the Excavating and Taking Inventory of Your Gifts Instructions**, and note that Tool 5 may take five days to complete. So this lesson will likely be more time-consuming than any of the previous lessons. And one step will require calling, emailing, or meeting with a friend or family member. Plan ahead by sending a note to the one you plan to connect with early in the week. Also, because Lesson 5 is pretty labor-intensive, let group members know that there will be more work time than usual in the next session, but not to let that stop them from putting in the amount of time they need to in between meeting times. Remember, the goal is progress at a pace that is consistent. **Read aloud "Closing" of Lesson 4.**

7. Dismiss.

Meeting Session 6: The workload for Lesson 5 was robust. It is likely that many people didn't make it through all parts of **Tool 5: Excavating and Taking Inventory of Your Gifts.** Welcome everyone by letting them know that this session will mostly be work time. Remember, the goal is progress at a pace that is consistent.

1. **Meet and Greet.** Connect with one another on the most basic things that make up your life—jobs, kids, husbands, pets, etc.

2. **Pray.** This is crucial. Invite the Holy Spirit to be present. Allow for silence as you wait upon his presence to be felt and revealed.

3. **Discuss the Reflection & Application Questions.** Each lesson includes a set of questions at the end of the Reflection & Application section. These will be your starting point each week. (If the group is larger than six people, split into small groups at this time.) **At this meeting, discuss Lesson 5, Reflection & Application questions.**

4. **Individual Processing and Reflection Time: Allow 45–60 minutes of work time during this meeting session to either catch up or move forward.** (See meeting session 3 instructions, above, for more details.)

5. **Share Progress Made with the Tool of the Lesson.** Each lesson has a tool—a set of instructions to complete an assignment designed to help each person *Go & See* her unique design. Each person shares the progress she has made and any insights she has gleaned. **At this meeting, share any one or two of the following and what you're beginning to see about your unique design from them:**
   5.1 Experiences Reflection Grid
   5.2 Excavating Calling Grid
   5.3 What Others See In You Post-Conversation Reflection
   5.4 Spiritual Gifts Inventory & Reflection Guide + Reflection Questions
   5.5 Processing Your Personality Type Grid
   5.6 Your Unique Artifact

6. **Read the Closing.** Briefly overview Lesson 6. Note that Tool 6: My Faith Family Tree is not nearly as much to process as Lesson 4 or 5. Whew! Remind the group that people on the tree need not be related to them or even Christians in order to have had an impact on their faith. There is an example on the last page of the lesson to help give a visual and ideas. **Read aloud "Closing" of Lesson 5.**

7. Dismiss.

Meeting Session 7: Sessions 7–9 are structured much the same as Lesson 2, and the workload for these is much less than for Lesson 5 and Lesson 6. The aim is to take all that deep digging from earlier lessons and apply what we have found in *Going & Seeing* to our lives by making plans of action. Some people struggle more to look back; others struggle more to look forward. So know that these next lessons may be easier for some and much harder for others.

1. **Meet and Greet.** Connect with one another on the most basic things that make up your life—jobs, kids, husbands, pets, etc.

2. **Pray.** This is crucial. Invite the Holy Spirit to be present. Allow for silence as you wait upon his presence to be felt and revealed.

3. **Discuss the Reflection & Application Questions.** Each lesson includes a set of questions at the end of the Reflection & Application section. These will be your starting point each week. (If the group is larger than six people, split into small groups at this time.) **At this meeting, discuss Lesson 6, Reflection & Application questions.**

4. **Share Progress Made with the Tool of the Lesson.** Each lesson has a tool—a set of instructions to complete an assignment designed to help each person *Go & See* her unique design. Each person shares the progress she has made and any insights she has gleaned. **At this meeting, share your Faith Family Tree, and what you saw while putting it together.**

5. **Individual Processing and Reflection Time: Allow 30–45 minutes of work time during this meeting session to either catch up or move forward**. (See meeting session 3 instructions for more details.)
6. **Read the Closing**. Briefly overview Lesson 7, and let the group know they'll be making action plans this week. The reading is much lighter than most weeks, but it may take quite a bit of solitude and waiting on the Lord to work through Tool 8: Relationship Investment Plan. Plan to start the Tool early so you have time to pray, think, and hear from the Lord prior to putting names down. **Read aloud "Closing" of Lesson 6**.
7. Dismiss.

Meeting Session 8: This session is very similar to session 7. The aim is to take all that deep digging from earlier lessons and apply what we have found in *Going & Seeing* to our lives by making plans of action. Some people struggle more to look back; others struggle more to look forward. It is also a time for anyone who is behind to *go* back and finish something that was skipped earlier.

1. **Meet and Greet**. Connect with one another on the most basic things that make up your life—jobs, kids, husbands, pets, etc.
2. **Pray**. This is crucial. Invite the Holy Spirit to be present. Allow for silence as you wait upon his presence to be felt and revealed.
3. **Discuss the Reflection & Application Questions**. Each lesson includes a set of questions at the end of the Reflection & Application section. These will be your starting point each week. (If the group is larger than six people, split into small groups at this time.) **At this meeting, discuss Lesson 7, Reflection & Application questions**.
4. **Share Progress Made with the Tool of the Lesson**. Each lesson has a tool—a set of instructions to complete an assignment designed to help each person *Go & See* her unique design. Each person shares the progress she has made and any insights she has gleaned. **At this meeting, share your Relationship Investment Plan, and what you saw while putting it together**.
5. **Individual Processing and Reflection Time: Allow 30–45 minutes of work time during this meeting session to either catch up or move forward.** (See meeting session 3 instructions for more details.)
6. **Read the Closing**. Briefly overview Lesson 8, and let the group know they'll be culminating all that they have taken the time to *Go & See* in a document that outlines their Purpose, Vision, and Values, as determined by seeing their (1) personal history, (2) unique design (spiritual gifts, natural talents, & personality type), and (3) relationships. This is fun! It can become a guiding document for learning how to say yes or no to opportunities. The examples included are a guide to get ideas, but the format doesn't need to be followed. **Read aloud "Closing" of Lesson 7**.
7. Dismiss.

Meeting Session 9: Wow! You made it. Time to celebrate. This session is very similar to session 5. And it is also meant to be a celebration. So if you can add anything to the night to celebrate this journey your group has walked, go for it. Make it fun and affirming!

1. **Meet and Greet**. Connect with one another on the most basic things that make up your life—jobs, kids, husbands, pets, etc.

2. **Pray**. This is crucial. Invite the Holy Spirit to be present. Allow for silence as you wait upon his presence to be felt and revealed.

3. **Gather Your Thoughts**. Allow a few minutes for people to review their Purpose, Vision, and Values documents and mentally and emotionally prepare to share them.

4. **Partner Sharing Time.** Find a partner, and each share your Purpose, Vision, and Values document. (No commentary, just read what is written.)

5. **Group Sharing Time**. After nerves have been worked out in the partner sharing, gather everyone together. If your group is larger than fifteen people, split into two small groups for this. If not, remain together as a larger group. Allow time for everyone to share their Purpose, Vision, and Values document. Not everyone has to share, but make sure not to stop this early. Long silences are okay. Some people need them to muster up the courage to share.

6. **Party & Farewell**: Create time and space for your group members to say farewell to one another, exchange contact info to stay in touch, and also express what was most helpful to them about the study.

7. Dismiss.

Acknowledgments

This book would not be in your hands without the support, sacrifice, and generosity of many more than I can name. Writing in and of itself is a solitary activity, but every one of those silent moments is made possible because of the people who have given me the courage, space, and confidence to pull away and put words to paper. When I flip through these pages, I see this not as an accomplishment of my own but that of a village of people with whom I have been blessed to share this journey called life.

To the ones I get to share my home with: Mike, thank you for your constant and consistent support and encouragement—even when I wanted to throw in the towel on this project (or others) you were there reminding me that God made me for a purpose and to press into that no matter what. Jacob, Moriah, Elim Jo, and Nathan (JeeWoo), I love capturing you using your God-given gifts. Each of you has a unique and splendid design, and I cannot wait to watch you discover and grow into the largeness of it.

To all my friends, literally across the globe, who have spurred me on: Thanks for reading the words, providing feedback, and most of all being present in my life in ways that have provided me wisdom, motivation, and encouragement. Most of all, thank you for listening and reminding me of who I am in Christ.

To all the Go & See Retreat attendees: Thank you for sacrificing your time and resources to spend a weekend away with me, exploring the content of this book. Watching your eyes light up, seeing visions come to life, and hearing your stories catalyzed this project forward. Your bravery and honesty continue to inspire me to keep using my gifts to help others Go & See how God has designed them for such a time as this.

To Kristal Bomstad: This book would be just words and clip art without your help. Thank you for undertaking bringing this book to life, even with my limited instructions and lack of design knowledge. You added the beauty I prayed would show up on its pages.

To Jordyn Marie Marshall: Thank you for capturing the one photo in this book that I pray every reader comes back to when she or he is needing a reminder of the saving grace of Jesus—the one who washes us clean and sets our hearts of stone beating again.

To my parents, David and Janet Malone: I would not be the person I am today without you. You introduced me to Jesus, hard work and living a life worthy of the calling. When I was young, I had no idea how much effort and sacrifice you put into creating a life for us that built our faith and confidence. Mom, this book is mostly for you because you are the one who never shrank back from letting me know that I "should write a book" about _____ (fill in the blank with a pertinent topic of faith or living for Jesus). Most days, I am not even sure this book was my idea but more an act of obedience to Jesus and follow-through on your recommendations.

To my siblings: Thanks for being awesome! And marrying awesome people who love Jesus and our family well. I am confident that I would not be who I am without having been raised alongside each of you as well as having the true blessing of calling each of you friends these many years later.

Finally, but most important, thank you to the Father, Son, and Holy Spirit. I am nothing and have nothing to bring the world outside of your love, sacrifice, and presence. When I haven't felt seen, your Word and presence reminds me of the truth that I am. When I have felt like giving up, your strength inside me has enabled me to fix my eyes. Thank you for the unique set of gifts you have given me to bless the world around me. Thank you also for your grace and forgiveness for the times I have held back or hidden behind excuses or fear. Thank you for inviting me into your mission on this earth and equipping me to be a light in the places you have predestined my feet to go. Jesus, you are the best. Thank you for nourishing my soul through asking me to bring you the "fish and loaves" I found when you asked me to *go* and *see*. You are good. And you are good to me. I love you.

Printed in the United States
By Bookmasters